Longmans' sociology of education

From three to thirteen
Socialization and achievement in school

Longmans' sociology of education

From three to thirteen
Socialization and achievement in school

J A Simms
Cambridge Institute of Education

and

T H Simms
Homerton College, Cambridge

Longmans

Longmans, Green and Co Ltd
London and Harlow

*Associated companies branches and representatives
throughout the world*

© *Longmans, Green and Co Ltd, 1969*

First published 1969

1058232436x

Set in and printed in Great Britain by
C. Tinling & Co. Ltd., Prescot

We are grateful to the students in the
Diploma Courses for Primary Education at the
Cambridge Institute of Education and to the
students of Saffron Walden College for some of
their observations of children's behaviour.

Contents

A*

Part 3 The child from nine to thirteen

Introduction

The argument of this book is that the social development of children is an important contributory factor to their individual achievement. Their levels of success in mastering physical and mental skills, and in the acquisition of knowledge, are profoundly influenced by the kinds of social experiences they have had. These experiences differ, and to understand them, an analysis must be made of the many variables, psychological and sociological, which interact in social situations common to ordinary children. Their families, their groups of friends, their teachers and their classes in school provide the opportunities for social development, through which they learn social competence and attain success in their school activities. Their successes occur in situations which both influence their social and personal development and feed back into their achievement.

The common stages of social and mental development among children of primary school age do not conform closely to the traditional divisions of children into the age ranges of infant, junior and secondary schools. The treatment of children's development in this book is therefore divided into three stages which reflect more nearly the important characteristics of their development. These are the pre-school years; the years from five to nine; the years from nine to thirteen.

Part I

The pre-school child

The enrichment of human life is a process by which each man learns to satisfy the needs and just claims of those with whom he is in contact, close or remote, and at the same time learns how to satisfy his own needs and strivings. It is the process by which his own development is achieved through a commitment to the development of other people. The newly born infant is helpless, inarticulate and a prey to impulses, but he is furnished with a rudimentary equipment with which to get to know his world. By the time he is ready for his first experience of school he has laid the foundations upon which the building of his mature personality and knowledge can take place. He has been engaged in complex learning which has enabled him to achieve motor control, walking and physical independence. He has learned to express his own feelings, to persuade people to do the things he wants and to order his understanding of his physical and social environment. He is learning to defer the satisfaction of his impulses. He has established primitive schemata or frameworks of knowledge with which to interpret the information provided by his senses. He has acquired the skills demanded of him by his age, sex role and the socio-economic milieu into which he has been born.

How this development takes place is the subject of exploration in the first part of this book.

1

The socialization of the pre-school child

At the moment of birth the child enters upon an immediate and absorbing relationship with two other people, his mother and his father. When he comes into existence he creates a new social unit, the family, which consists of a complex of interrelationships between himself, his parents and the other children.[1] The family as a social unit is remarkable for the variety of forms in which the inherent authority of the adult parents over the dependent children may be expressed. At the same time no other social unit is capable of such close affectional ties as may exist between the members of a family.

For the child both affection and authority are personified in his father and mother. The distribution of authority between his parents, their attitudes towards each other and their conceptions of their affectional roles in relation to each other as well as to himself have a profound effect upon his personal development.

The role of the mother in satisfying the child's earliest needs gives her primary importance. Through her handling of the child and the quality of her mothering he learns the meaning of security and the beginnings of confidence. In these, as Bowlby has shown, the mother's affectional relationship with the child is highly important for his subsequent development.[2] The father is traditionally the personification of authority within the family. He provides a model, particularly for his son, who learns his own sex role through contact with the ways in which it is embodied in his father's characteristics and behaviour. In the contemporary family such simple separation of roles is not to be found. In some families rehousing has led to the break up of wider family networks and the creation of more isolated family units in which major decisions are taken jointly by both parents.

3

In other families where the mothers are at work it has followed that the father has taken over some of the affectional ties and routine duties normally regarded as part of the mother's role. Each young child's family environment provides a complex of variables enabling only partial generalizations to be made about the effects of the varying roles of parents. It has been found, for example, that where the mother is the dominant figure boys grow up and respond to stress with self-blame and anxiety. Girls in the same situation are more dependable but some evidence suggests they may develop over-great control and find it difficult to establish relationships with boys. Where the father maintains his traditional role boys show greater aggression and initiative and show the beginnings of some quality of leadership. Even such a simple relationship between the parent and the child is complicated by another variable: that of the approval or disapproval of the other parent which each communicates to the children. It has been suggested that if a dominant mother tends to depreciate the father's role, the daughters might tend to devalue men, and the sons might have difficulty in identification with their father, with consequent problems in their adjustment to their sex role.[3]

An important variable is the size of the family in which the child is born. Each child has a unique position in the order of the siblings. Parents are naturally concerned with the firstborn and they have time to give him their sole attention. As a result he is likely to suffer a more intense displacement experience than the younger children. Younger children have models for learning their age and sex roles provided by older siblings. It must also be remembered that in a large family the parents themselves are older when the youngest children are born. The significance of these effects of position in the family have not been sufficiently explored for firmly grounded statements to be made about the relationship between position in family and size of family, and the socialization of the children. Although there is evidence that the mean I.Q. of smaller families is higher than that of larger families, this may reflect socio-economic status rather than family size as such. It has been found, for example, that the eldest children in middle-class families show a greater desire to succeed than their siblings. The eldest children of working-class families show the opposite tendency.[4]

Although it is difficult to relate cause and effect among the variables which make up a family situation, the essential uniqueness of that complex we call the family unit is demonstrated by Dr J. G. Howells's view that whenever a child patient is presented for psychiatric treatment, it becomes necessary to examine and treat the whole family, for the child's deviant behaviour is frequently no more than a symptom of family relationships which have gone wrong.[5]

From the comparatively limited environment of the family which includes grandparents, aunts, uncles, baby-sitters and the like, each with their different roles to play, the child moves normally into the company of his friends from other families. These groups provide a further reinforcement of what he has learned in the family and other challenges in which further learning takes place. At this age he is more likely to be interested in play material than in a contemporary except in so far as a contemporary frustrates his play. By one and a half years the play materials provide a bridge between contemporaries, and cooperative play occurs with increasing frequency and intensity from about three years onwards. In order to achieve successful play he is learning how cooperation with other children will help him to satisfy his needs.[6] To satisfy his existing need for acceptance he has already learnt a number of simple social skills operative within the family setting: how to smile, to cry with a purpose, and to draw attention to himself. Now in the wider setting of other children he extends his learning to cope with the more complex situations they present. He learns to master the skills that group play demands, to follow its rules, and to show off, as in this example:

Helen, 3 years, 6 months, is playing with her brothers, Paul, 8 years, and Mark, 6 years. They are in the boys' bedroom and are playing with Mark's collection of zoo animals. Helen looks at Paul and says, 'You haven't set it out yet.' 'You help,' says Paul. Helen picks up a baby lion in her right hand and bangs it on the bed post, 'I am a little baby lion and I sit on a little roof. Bang! Bang!' The baby lion falls to the floor. 'Look how it landed.' She picks it up and puts it in her mouth. She is still standing on the fringe watching the boys play. She puts down the lion and picks up the rhinoceros saying, 'What kind of noise do they make?' Mark makes a spluttering noise. Helen, "It doesn't say anything." Her attention returns to the rhinoceros. She picks it up in her right hand and says, 'I don't know where to feed her.' Paul says, 'There is a silver dish in the farm.' She climbs over the bed and returns with a tin lid which she puts in the rhinoceros' imaginery play 'field'. She then places the rhinoceros with its head over the dish as if feeding. She moves a keeper and says, 'Put that one there.' Mark picks up a wild boar and says, 'Hoggy.' Helen repeats, 'Hoggy, hoggy—isn't he a nice hoggy?' Paul says, 'It is a wild boar.' Helen says, 'Wild boar, I mean.' Helen watches the boys and appears to follow their conversation carefully. She moves the dish, and puts the smaller rhinoceros to drink at the dish. She picks up the large rhinoceros and says, 'Hello, how are you today? This is a baby rhinoceros, and this is a daddy rhinoceros.' Paul says, 'I'll knock them over.' Helen replies vigorously, 'Oh no! You dare! I'll run round,' and she quickly moves the rhinoceros round the 'field'. She sits back on her heels watching and listening to the boys again. She picks up the two rhinoceroses, one in each hand, 'They've eaten all their food.'

The family not only provides an immediate environment of close and continuing relationships between its members but is itself set in an environment of forces which are mediated through it to each child in the family. Although it is possible to categorize families as nuclear, consisting of mother, father, and one or more children, or as extended, consisting of mother, father, children and close relations by blood and marriage living near and playing a significant part in the life of the family, most families contain, in varying degrees, elements of both the nuclear and extended family. Every family, of whatever size, has some relationships with other members of its own kin. It has also a relationship with the world of work through the father's instrumental role as a wage earner. It is related to the neighbourhood through a widening circle of acquaintances whose opinions help to shape the values of the family.

The traditions of the family are mediated from the older members to the child through their stories of the past. A professional family may attempt to hand on the standards and values which have marked the successful careers of uncles, grandfathers, or ancestors even more remote. The role of women in such families has in the past been to maintain a standard of expectation for their men, although in the last generation a number of them have reinforced the family traditions by their own achievements in the professions. In humbler families the tradition may express itself differently. The folklore of the grandmother becomes the groundwork for the mother's advice to her daughter in the major crises of life, birth, illness and death.[7]

In every occupation the father's work provides an opportunity for the children to learn something of the objectivity which characterizes economic activities. Punctual working hours or the demands of overtime bring the child into contact with more impersonal forces than any within the family itself.

As the father is set in the context of work so the family is set in the context of the neighbourhood. The neighbourhood may provide a face-to-face relationship with people who reinforce the standards and outlook of the family. It may provide only a window-to-window relationship, but even here the implicit assumptions of the neighbours exercise a powerful influence. The occupation of his father and the standards of his neighbourhood contribute to a child's picture of the world outside his family. They lead him to acquire patterns of behaviour and attitudes appropriate to the socio-economic status of his family. They mediate to the child the different modes of conduct associated with the subcultures they represent.

Surrounding the family there exist spheres of relationship which reach out into the whole community. These wider influences, already interpreted and modified by the older members of the family, are embodied for the child in visits to places and meeting people, in hearing talk about events, in looking at pictures, and as he begins to read, in the material provided by comics and books. But more important than his knowledge is his wider experience of personal relationships. He has more people to admire, respect and imitate so that, when he comes to school, he may be ready for an extension of the identification process to the teacher.

He may accept the conditions she embodies for success in school. He is by the age of five the centre of a complex of forces originating at first within the family and widening to take in those of society at large.

2

Socialization and the development of personality

The young child is not moulded by such external factors as those of the family and society without himself taking an active part in the process of his own development. Children's responses to the multiplicity of stimulation afforded by their environment will vary according to their temperamental differences, the ways in which they have learnt to perceive, and their feelings of pleasure or displeasure arising from the occasion. The interplay of the active child with his social and physical environment enables those modifications of his own endowment which we call adaptation to take place. From the earliest stages there are beginning to develop more or less established emotional and behavioural response patterns appropriate to the people and things that matter to him. These may be called attitudes. The foundations of these attitudes are laid in the emotionality of the child. The child's emotional endowment is at first undifferentiated. It has an all-or-nothing quality. With maturation and experience come emotional differentiation and a greater stability of response as the patterns of hormonal stimulation and their accompanying bodily changes are established.[1] This consistency of reaction is expressed in behaviour associated with feeling that enables the process of attitude formation to develop.

The growth of attitudes takes place in a social context which determines their strength and direction. Three major psychological states may be identified as a result of the child's interaction with his social environment. These are dependency, aggression and anxiety. Their importance lies in the contribution they make to the pattern of a child's attitudes. Dependency is a form of behaviour which takes place whenever a child turns to other people as a source of nurturance. Aggression is goal-seeking behaviour directed to the injury of another person. Anxiety is a generalized state of feeling which often involves a tendency to take avoiding action to reduce that state. Each of these is a complex of feeling and behaviour that demands fuller treatment.

Dependency

Dependency arises from the biological helplessness of the human infant whose every want can only be satisfied through the actions of an adult, who is usually his mother. Normal mothers respond to their infant's physical needs with further gratifications expressed in touch, sounds and smiles. The infant of six months has learned to seek such responses from his mother through his own smiles and cries. Since the reinforcement of his behaviour depends upon his mother's responses to his signals, the quality of his reinforcement depends upon the quality of her mothering. The continued reinforcement leads to a relationship between the infant and his mother which provides him with a physical gratification. It is at the same time a psychological gratification. In his search for this psychological gratification the infant has already learned some elementary techniques to evoke the relationship of dependency. Little is known about the reasons why children seem to vary in the strength and frequency of their dependency behaviour. Nevertheless it is clear that when conflict arises between the child's expectancy of mothering behaviour and the mother's failure to give it, a state of anxiety arises which leads him to search even more actively for dependency gratification.

Infantile dependency has for its natural objects the mother and, in due course, the father. As the child's awareness of his social environment grows so the number of people with whom he can enter upon a dependency relationship increases. This takes place at first within the family, with older brothers and sisters, and gradually extends to adults outside the home and to children chosen from those of his own age. At the same time his repertoire of behaviour widens to enable him to replace the simpler forms of attention seeking by more sophisticated and elaborate patterns. A baby who seeks to be cuddled is likely to develop into a child whose physical feats and intellectual accomplishments are the means by which he seeks the approval of his peers or older people:

Diane, 4 years, 4 months, engaged in painting looked at the adult and said, 'I'm getting some water.' She smiled at the adult. 'Look, I'm washing them.' She then showed her picture and said, 'Is that nice?'

While the evidence is at present meagre, it does seem safe to suggest that the consistent affection, approval and support of the dependency figure for the child enable him to cope with new situations and strive to be successful in them. However, patterns of dependency behaviour may lead to quite different outcomes. On the one hand a child whose behaviour is characterized by over-great dependency is likely to show some degree of conformity with adult and group norms.[2] On the other hand later aggressive and anti-social acts have been traced to the inadequate satisfaction of dependency needs because of inconsistent responses on the part of the adult to the child's behaviour.[3]

Aggression

A second factor influencing the emotional development of the child is aggression. Aggressive behaviour arises when the child is frustrated in attaining his goal and it is marked by a desire to remove and injure the person who is preventing him from attaining his end. Such a person is depriving him of the reinforcement which would accompany successful achievement. It is at first an unlearned response. In early childhood the anger response is total; it is one in which the whole body and voice are involved. Outbursts of anger have been found to increase up to eighteen months. Boys consistently tend to show a greater incidence of such outbursts than girls. Up to two years of age the child physically expresses his anger towards other people and his playthings. Between two and six years with increased verbal facility he finds new forms of expressing aggression. The incidence of frustration does not decline, because parental restrictions continue to accompany the increasing socialization of the child through toilet training, behaviour at meals and the sharing of toys.[4] Children who are highly active are exposed to a wider range of frustrations caused by their explorations. They become agents of their own frustrations and are more likely to express them in destructive play. The situation is accentuated if legitimate outlets have not been offered through the provision of such play materials as clay, dough, and hammering toys:

Ian, 3 years, 11 months, showed very little open display of aggression in his play. Then one interesting example was shown when Kevin, 3 years, 3 months, attempted to join in the train play. Ian snatched two trucks and held them and deliberately disconnected the track so that Kevin could not use it. When the teacher was called to the rescue Ian liked telling her, 'It came off itself.' After this however he seemed more ready to accept Kevin into the game and parallel play ensued.

In seeking to injure people or their property the nature of the aggressive response is essentially destructive. Every social culture has realized the need for approving of certain responses and disapproving of others according to their effect upon the stability of the society. The psychological mechanism by which this process is achieved is through identification and modelling. In normal family relationships the chief aggressive model is the father. An aggressive adult has a twofold effect upon a child. He increases the incidence of aggressive responses on the part of the child and he provides him with examples of new forms of aggression which the child learns to make his own.[5]

A considerable element of physical and verbal aggression is found in the behaviour of children from families where physical and verbal threats provide the sanctions for child-rearing practices. The following recorded behaviour of a group of children in a nursery school, from families of low socio-economic status, shows marked overt aggressive behaviour:

Paul, 4 years, 8 months. Paul is in the trolley being pushed by Stephen, 4 years. They pass a group of boys. Stephen chases the three boys away, while Paul remains seated in the trolley.

Paul, 'I'll frow a spear at you.' He makes a movement of throwing his spear and shouts, 'I'll frow a spear at you, Alwyn.' He climbs out of the trolley, runs up to Alwyn, pretends to stab him, and returns to the trolley. Stephen, Alwyn and the rest continue the mock fight. Paul watches from the trolley and calls, 'See, I'll kill you, boy. Come on, Stephen.' A small boy (not Stephen) detaches himself from the group and begins to climb on the trolley. Paul, 'Ge' off it.' The small boy moves away. Paul to Stephen, 'Come on.' Stephen has hurt his leg in the battle and approaches the trolley looking tearful. Evidently Alwyn is blamed. Paul, 'Alwyn come 'ere—I'll kill you.' Paul gets out of the trolley and goes up to Alwyn who is near Stephen. He catches hold of Alwyn and to Stephen says, ' 'It 'im.' Stephen does so. Paul steps into it. Stephen looks sad. Paul, 'Do you want to come, Steve?' Stephen approaches Paul. Paul, 'When you ketch 'im I'll 'it 'im in the face. You ketch 'im, I'll 'it 'im.' By this time Alwyn has disappeared. Paul, 'Let's get Alwyn.' They run on the grass. Paul, 'Here's 'at Alwyn? We say we've got to get 'im. I know where 'e is, 'e must be in school.' At this point they are distracted by seeing a dog in the grass and start to chase it.

Children of higher socio-economic classes acquire through their greater command of language a wider repertoire of responses which enables them to accept the inhibitory effect of the modelling of the adults in this group.[6] Such generalizations are, of course, modified for each individual child by other variables. It has been found, for example, that the establishment of strong friendships between pairs of nursery school children leads to a redirection of aggressive behaviour away from each other and towards their teacher. A child's response to frustration may be changed according to the pattern of social relationships in which he finds himself.[7]

The frustration of dependency by adults either failing to reinforce a child's behaviour or doing so inconsistently is a frequent cause of aggressive responses. Where the child does not know whether what he does receives parental approval or not, he loses confidence in his ability to cope with the events and the relationships of his family life. This leads to a state of anxiety. To this some children react by withdrawal and apathy and others by forms of aggressive and antisocial behaviour.

Anxiety

Dependent responses and aggressive acts are similar in that they can be observed. Anxiety falls into a different category for it is a state of mind which need not be expressed in observable acts. Nevertheless it has an important effect upon human behaviour.[8] It may be aroused by a wide range of stimuli or limited to specific situations. It has an energizing effect, leading to the avoidance of the tension-producing situation. The avoiding action may be positive, leading to a heightened skill in disposing of, or substituting an alternative way of dealing with the threat situation. A number of different situations, or a combination of them, may produce a state of anxiety in a young child. These may be separation from his mother; a lack of warmth in her mothering; a threat to his physical safety; a strange social setting; or the fear of punishment and frustration. As cognitive development takes place, the objects which, at two years of age, were novel and harmless become, at the age of four, stimuli which arouse fear, the general unpleasant feelings of anxiety associated with specific stimuli:

Jill, 3 years, 3 months, lived near an aerodrome and was already familiar with aeroplanes. As she was playing with her dolls one day, she heard an obtrusive aeroplane, and suddenly ran across to her mother burying her head in her lap. This was a novel response subsequently repeated on similar occasions.

In order to cope with such situations the child learns a variety of ways of avoiding them or adapting himself to avoid the worst effects of these unpleasant experiences. Success in adjusting to these events is a function of his previous experiences, his level of maturation, the way in which he has learned to cope with similar situations and his constitutional qualities. His anxieties are revealed through his bodily movement and subsequently in his use of materials and toys. Through these he can play out fantasies which enable him to come to terms with his anxieties and frustrations. He achieves his goals by the substitution of fantasy objects, which he can manipulate, for the real sources of his anxiety:

Jacqueline, 4 years, 11 months, had painted a large house and garden without figures. She looked at the painting and said, 'The little girl is running down the street, there's a witch chasing her. Her mummy is standing at the gate, so the little girl goes in and her mummy shuts the gate, bang. The witch can't get in.'

As a child's environment widens so he is presented with new tasks and problems which offer him immediate short term goals. Through successfully tackling these, he learns the satisfaction of achievement. Initial failure, accompanied by anxiety, drives him to repeated efforts and final success, so that the anxiety is reduced. The supporting role of the adult favours the reduction of anxiety:

Robert, 3 years, 6 months, liked his father to accompany him into nursery school as far as his peg. He showed some diffidence at leaving his father until he had looked into the nursery. Once this had happened he walked into the room without a backward look.

Anxiety arises when the dependency needs of the child are not satisfied or when his aggressive outbursts are not accompanied by the learning which will help him to come to terms with them. These three factors in the emotional life of the child are of crucial importance in his future development. With the help of supporting and understanding adults, he can develop the confidence and skills with which to tackle new situations outside the home. Such adults enable him to come to terms with emotional forces which are too great for him to cope with alone.

3

The development of attitudes

The child's dependency needs, aggressive acts and anxiety states lay the foundations for the development of attitudes. These involve a general readiness to respond favourably or unfavourably to aspects of the environment.[1] There are four aspects towards which the development of favourable attitudes leads to successful achievement. These are other children, adults in authority, himself, and work. In his early and not yet firmly crystallized attitudes to these four elements in his world are laid the foundations of success or failure in his adaptation to the social and intellectual demands of school.

Attitude to others

The child's first social relationships with his parents develop from their satisfaction of his needs. When he first comes into contact with other young children, their egocentricity makes it impossible for him to find his needs satisfied through them. The child at home has already mastered some skills through the toys that the family has provided for him, but when he enters a group of children in a nursery where he finds a wider range of play material, he is likely to continue as an individual to discover the opportunities afforded by it. His use of material may at the same time be accompanied by his observation of other children, or by sharing the same material with them, but following his independent line of play.[2] Gradually he comes to realize that certain equipment, like the swing in the nursery or the box in the street, can best be exploited through making contact with other children:

Julian, 3 years, 11 months, showed considerable ingenuity in leadership when he acted as voluntary driver on the round. was sure of himself as driver and made no offer to change places with anyone else using this apparatus.

Sharon, 3 years, 6 months, is in the driving seat of the indoor roundabout. Her friend Patricia is in the passenger seat. Douglas comes up and pushes their backs as they revolve. Sharon, 'You lot get off. You lot can't push. I'm making you go round Patricia.' To Douglas, 'Do you want me to chop your head off?' 'We don't want any more, Douglas. Don't you dare, Douglas, I'll cut your bum off.' As Douglas stops pushing, 'Push us again, Dougie. Push us again, Dougie. No more, Dougie.'

The compelling attraction of the play situation is approached in a variety of ways, shy, aggressive, confident or cautious. These different ways are derived from variations in the psychological consequences of the child-rearing practices in the home and the child's reaction towards them, his own temperament, his opportunities for social experience and his capacity to order them in language.

Language plays a crucial part not only in expressing but also in fostering the social relationships of children. The acquisition of language from parents and siblings develops into a capacity for formulating the verbal expression of motor and emotional responses. When therefore a child is engaged in solitary or parallel play, it is not unlikely that he will be engaged in a running commentary on his activities. This commentary stabilizes the sequence of his actions, increases his power of discriminating betwen them and equips him with a vocabulary and rules for sentences appropriate to the activities he is engaged in:

Ian, 3 years, 11 months. It seemed that when Ian had become proficient in the motor skill of pushing the engine and truck round the track, he was able to verbalise his actions. 'Now I'm coming down this and I've stopped.' On the other hand a complete sentence might be used to indicate a future action, perhaps showing that language had begun to motivate his actions. 'I'm going to go over this hill.' 'I want to make it go faster.' This use of language was an active one, concerned with doing both in the present and in the future.

At the same time a child's use of language is helping him to develop his powers of acquiring concepts. At first the word he has learnt is applied to a concrete object with all its particular characteristics. Later as he appreciates the identity and consistency of objects regardless of their changing perceptual appearances, so he is moving toward the mastery of the principle of conservation. The word comes to express the essential features of the object, for it ignores the non-essential details.[3]

Jennifer, 2 years, 2 months, was drinking her bedtime milk sitting on her own little chair. 'Daddy's chair; Mummy's chair; Jennifer's chair. Daddy's loo; Mummy's loo; Jennifer's potty. Jennifer's bed; Daddy's bed, with Mummy in it.'

The establishment of concepts and of word signals for them (like those Jennifer was engaged in mastering), provides the child with an instrument which enables him to establish communication with other children about the actions that they are undertaking and the objects they are concerned with, whether in parallel or co-operative play. Through the use of concepts and signals he imposes order upon his environment. He has established a framework which enables him to approach other children who in turn have also acquired similar frameworks to deal with their common world:

Deborah, 4 years, 6 months, assigns the roles which make up a family group and avoids a possible clash with Tony which might threaten the play: Deborah leaves the ironing board and comes to the table, near which are Tony, 4 years, 8 months, Mary, 4 years, 2 months, and Ivan, 3 years, 4 months. She says to Ivan, 'I'm mummy, you're daddy.' Tony protests, 'I'm daddy.' Deborah agrees, 'He's daddy, you're boy, she's auntie.'

A week later, Deborah, 4 years, 6 months, Karen, 4 years, 6 months, Mary, 4 years, 2 months, were putting on their outdoor clothes in order to play outside. Deborah picked up her shoulder bag, 'This is mine, this is mine.' Karen asked, 'Who's baby?' Mary, 'I'm not baby!' Karen of Mary, 'She can be little girl.' Deborah, 'She's too small,' To Mary, 'You're little baby.' Then quickly to Karen, 'She's little baby, Karen.'

A readiness to approach other children, reinforced by the contacts available through the use of language, leads to attempts to play with other children, to experiments in aggressive behaviour, in friendly domination or willing submission. When the children begin to find satisfaction in group play, the emergence of a group feeling begins to take place. This stage introduces a new significance into the social relationships of children for group play involves the acceptance of many forms of behaviour in the course of the play. During the play each child's behaviour is determined by the levels of domination and persistence he displays. A skilful use of language will strengthen his playing of the part. In family play, transport play, workmen play or special occasion play such as weddings and christenings, children discover many surprises in other children's reactions towards them and they learn that other children are personalities to be taken into account. They cope with these surprises by adjusting their responses to the expectations of others. They are learning to acquire a social flexibility which allows them to experiment in social relationships and to understand them. It enables a child to exercise control and purpose :

Diane, 4 years, 4 months. Frankie, a four-year-old spastic child, came and stood in a dangerous position near the swings. Diane who had been playing near the swings walked up to him, tried to encourage him to move saying, 'Come on Frankie, you'll get 'urt.' Frankie refused to move so Diane left him, walked towards the side of the swings and picked up the golliwog which she had left there. She walked back towards Frankie and offered him the golliwog, 'Come on Frankie, you can have my golly.' This failed to move Frankie in any way. Diane then took him by the hand and tried to lead him away. He was more heavily built than she and Diane had to tug, which she did gently saying, 'Come on Frankie, you'll get 'urt.' After a few seconds she was successful in leading Frankie to a place of safety.

Attitude to authority

Reference has already been made to the basic importance of the home in the early establishment of the emotional and social development of the child. It has been indicated that the family may be regarded from one point of view as the unit for the protection of its dependent members and as an instrument for the exercise of power on the part of its adult members. Whenever a child comes into contact with an adult he is in fact facing someone who is in a position of responsibility for him and therefore of authority over him. This interaction takes place within a cultural context. Parents' interpretations of authority are derived from their reactions to their own upbringing. Other adults such as uncles and aunts are likely to have accepted the broadly-based attitudes to the exercise of authority that are accepted in the social context in which the family is set. The pattern of emotional and behavioural responses the child develops towards the kind of authority exercised over him is the first stage in the formation of the way in which he will react to the subsequent exercise of authority. This pattern of responses becomes a pervading element in the development of his personality. The forms in which families exercise authority over their children range widely within similar social levels.[4] At one extreme are to be found the restricting influences associated with powerful parental domination; at the other extreme are the indulgent practices which stem from the parents' failure to interfere, or neglect. Between these extremes can be found a wide range of families which broadly adopt the principle of giving children freedom to operate within an acknowledged structure, as in the example below:

Helen, 3 years, 5 months, is having tea at the table with her mother, father and three elder siblings. Mother asks, 'Who would like a cup of tea?' Helen holds up her right hand and says, 'Yes please. Squash please.'
Mother, 'Do you really want squash, Helen?'
Helen, 'Yes.'
Mother, 'Pardon.'
Helen, 'Yes, please.' Mother makes two glasses of squash.
Helen, 'I want mine the fullest.'
Her mother gives her a buttered bun. She starts to lick the butter off.
Mother, 'Don't do that.' 'Why?' asks Helen. She continues licking.
Mother, 'Helen, stop!' Helen does so.
She says, 'Please can I not leave the table?' and laughs.
She eats the remainder of the bun and says, 'Finished!' and jumps down.

So many variables contribute to the differences in child-rearing practices that little accurate generalization can yet be made about their effects upon the personalities of children brought up under differing regimes. Yet in much educational and sociological writing there exist certain stereotypes of personality tied to social class variables in child-rearing practices. Hence it is important to indicate what relationships have been found in this field. Parents of every social class are concerned with those qualities that will ensure success in the roles they expect the child will fill, but the roles are likely to be determined by the class culture of the family. It has been found, for example, that middle-class parents take into account the child's motives and feelings and emphasize internalized standards of conduct such as honesty and self control. They use such methods as appeals to reason, or to guilt feelings, or withdrawal of affection. These non-physical measures are both compelling and effective. Though they may show a greater permissiveness in satisfying the child's needs and in emphasizing independence in early childhood, middle-class parents do not relax their pressures on their children towards achievement and success. The result is that middle-class children in a situation of conflict tend to develop skills which result in socially acceptable behaviour.[5]

Manual and unskilled working-class parents tend to look upon their children's behaviour in the light of its immediate consequences. In a conflict situation, manual working-class children tend to solve their problems in ways which show little use of previous experience, for each situation is treated pragmatically in terms of its consequence. This may hinder the development of a consistent attitude towards authority. Consistency seems to arise from the repetition of consequences rather than the internalization of principles. These differences between the classes are reinforced by the use of language. The structure of middle-class language allows for explanation and reasoning which help the child actively to participate in the conflict situation. A working-class family which has only a restricted form of language at its disposal tends to respond to cues which are limited only to the immediate present and the expression of authority exercised by the adult.[6] Already by the time a child has reached nursery school age, the foundations for these different uses of language have been laid in the sociocultural context in which he has been brought up.

One of the difficulties which accompanies all attempts to explore the relationship between social class and personality is the changing social structure of the last twenty-five years. With the decrease of manual labour, greater affluence and the consequent reduction in the cultural distance between status-aspiring working-class and middle-class parents, some of the divergences found in earlier studies have become less marked in more recent work. There has been a reduction in physical punishment, a gradual shift in the role of the father from being a figure of authority to becoming a companion to his children, and both parents share the dual role of authority and affection.[7] As the child develops towards readiness for school and wider contacts outside the family so he will approach new figures of authority with the patterns of response already reinforced in the home. The foundations have been laid for the emergence of those qualities in later life which William James called 'tough-mindedness' or 'tender-mindedness'. These qualities are revealed at an early age:

Elizabeth, 3 years, 6 months, was by the swing in the Nursery School garden. A woman visitor was sitting near.
Elizabeth, 'Push me! Push me!' The visitor did not look up.
Elizabeth, 'Push me! Push me then!' the visitor continued writing.
Elizabeth, 'Ladies push little girls. Push me. Push me.' No response from the visitor.
Elizabeth, 'Push me will you?'
'Just push me a minute.'
'Push me please. Push me will you?'
The visitor began to walk away. Elizabeth, 'You're not pushin' me. You're going going around.'
The visitor approached the swing and began to push Elizabeth. Elizabeth, 'Now you're pushin'. Now you're pushin'.'

In her repeated demands Elizabeth showed a persistent tough-mindedness.

Attitude to himself

It has been assumed so far that the child is capable of responding to the stimulation of his physical and social environment. The nature of his responses changes as maturation takes place. He begins to grow aware of himself as the agent of his responses. He cannot enter into the conscious experience of an infant but his behaviour shows that he does not at first regard himself as separate from his surroundings. During the sensori-motor stage there is no evidence that any mediating consciousness intervenes between the stimulus and the response. The first step towards self-identity is taken when the infant begins to recognize his body as separate from the existence of objects or persons in the outer reality. This is accompanied by a recognition of recurring experiences, possible only when the maturation of the cortex of the brain enables him to retain them. The awareness of a bodily self is reinforced by physical and psychological frustrations arising from objects and people in his environment. By the age of one and a half years the child has established the separation of his bodily self from the rest of the world.

Of fundamental importance to the growth of self-awareness is the acquisition of language. It provides the child with tools for relating his environment to himself. The most important of these instruments is the repetition of the child's own name which provides him with a clear and constantly recurring point of reference.[8] He is not only an independent member of the family but when he can name his toys, his parents, and his siblings he begins to find that whether they are present or absent, the one permanent factor is himself. The verbalization of relationships with others tend to crystallize his relationships with them and increases his self-identity as against others with whom he is in contact. The process is slow and confusion often reveals itself in speech or behaviour. He can also lose his self-identity in play, so that he finds it difficult to differentiate between himself and the objects of his fantasy.

The acquisition of one's name provides the self with a symbol around which strong emotions cluster; it becomes a vehicle for the strongest of them all, self-esteem. When a child's attempts to explore his environment are thwarted, often by well meaning adults who wish to help him, he feels his self-initiated activity blocked. One characteristic of this stage, about the age of two, is negativism. His response to adult proposals which seem to him to threaten the integrity of his self is expressed by "No". In such situations he is not necessarily developing anti-social behaviour; he is defending both his self-identity and self-esteem. The complexity of behaviour involving the self is shown in the following examples:

Ian, 3 years, 11 months, used language for several purposes, as a tool for self assertion and self awareness saying 'No' firmly several times to other children; as an expression of personal ability and prowess, 'I go fast.' 'I slowed down, didn't I?'; as an expression of ownership, 'That was mine, Nigel. That was mine.' In the latter case he used repetition of words instead of physical action, showing that he had realized their symbolic value.

Jennifer, 2 years, 4 months, was given a box of sweets by an adult friend. She opened the box and helped herself generously to three. Her father then said, 'Shall we put the box away, Jennifer?' She gave the box to her father, who put it upon a shelf. About an hour and a half later in a quiet interval between plays she asked for her 'box'. Her father gave the sweets but said, 'Wouldn't you like to hand the sweets round to everybody first, Jennifer?' In turn she offered the sweets to the three adult visitors and then took one herself. She did not offer her father the sweets. Having identified with him in this behaviour, it seemed that in satisfying herself she had satisfied him.

The emergence of an awareness of bodily self, continuing self-identity and self-esteem are not successive and completed stages but they continue to grow in complexity during the late pre-school years. As the child learns to manipulate the pronouns which differentiate him from others so his self-identity becomes clearer, and as the child acquires a sense of possession so his self-esteem is reinforced by self-extension; he owns his toys, his parents, his house. This rudimentary self-extension is accompanied by the beginnings of a self-picture. From the response of his parents he learns what their expectations are and by the time he is ready to go to school he can compare these expectations with his own behaviour. This process has been accelerated when the child has learned the meaning of the words "good boy", and can apply them to his own behaviour. He evaluates himself according to the norms implicit in these words; the judgment of others is part of learning to judge oneself:

Sharon, 3 years, 6 months, is running down five steps. As she runs down she calls out, 'Nigel you're a bad little boy.' At the bottom of the steps she slips and falls, but she continues to make her way back in order to run down the steps again. Two other three year olds are impeding her progress. She says to them, 'You lot get off. You lot, you can't push!' When neither of them moves, she starts chanting, 'You bad kids. You bad little kids.' She repeats this, then from the top of the steps she runs down again to the bottom.

The verbal reinforcement of the adult offers the first criterion by which the young child can assess the moral value of his acts and the moral standing of himself. This must take place within the context of a child's continuing dependency upon the adults around him in a relationship of either affection or of power. Their physical presence, the consistency of their modelling and their approval or withdrawal, within a supporting family environment, are necessary conditions for the child to establish a firm self-picture.[9]

Attitude to work

The use of the word 'play' in relation to a child's behaviour has little scientific value. It has been used as a description, as an explanation and as a justification of behaviour. Some writers have given it instrumental value; others an intrinsic value. It has been called 'an instinct' and 'energy releaser', 'a means of adjustment', 'a preparation for adult life'.[10] For our purposes perhaps the most useful approach to play is to compare it with language. As egocentric language is a commentary on the child's activities and fantasies, so egocentric play reveals the child's needs and feelings. Similarly as socialized language reveals the relationships that he is establishing with other people, so group play reveals the needs that can only be met through his contacts with other children. Both forms of play may well exist side by side.

The play activities of a healthy pre-school child help him to organize his world, to understand it by identifying himself with people and objects within it and by coming to terms with what he does not understand through fantasy or imitation. An overdependent child, an anxious child or a child who cannot come to terms with his aggressive impulses will reveal these in the form of his play and find through play a measure of accepting his dependency, his anxiety or his hostilities.

The observation of children of pre-school years gives concrete form to the concept of play. Their activities are marked by qualities of concentration. They solve problems and in doing so acquire skills. Attending to an object or situation implies selective perception in that the field from which sensory stimulation comes is limited. There is an increase in the span of attention during the pre-school years but it is doubtful as to what is responsible for this developmental process.[11] The selective nature of attention arises early; experience of the bottle, for example, may prepare the child to anticipate its appearance and to reach for it. According to Piaget the child learns to perceive through the interaction of his movements and sensory perceptions. At the age of three years he is still reinforcing visual perception by tactile and kinaesthetic perception and has reached the stage of perceiving and identifying common objects. By this time his sensory input is likely to be interpreted in terms of past experience and existing attitudes. The child explores the object through his senses, discovers its distinctive features and develops skill in attending to them. Recent evidence suggests that the sense of touch as a sole means of identifying objects develops later than the sense of sight and does not reach its full discriminating powers until the child is already at school.[12] It is in his play that a child reveals his powers of perceptual discrimination:

Alison, 2 years, 7 months, is looking at a picture magazine, turning over the pages.

'Baby's waiting for breakfast.' She correctly names the activity and identifies anticipation. 'Mummy's picked baby up.' She correctly names the activity.

In his play he also reveals his powers of concentration:

Ian, 3 years, 11 months.

During the first period of observation of Ian in the nursery school he changed rapidly from one piece of equipment to another. At first nothing seemed to occupy his attention for very long or to absorb him completely. He hardly repeated himself in the use of equipment during the first four observations. He seemed to work steadily through each example of apparatus.

As the child's powers of perception and attending are exercised on a wider range of objects in his environment, so his skill in perceiving and attending increases through the practice they afford him. The capacity to acquire new skills is a function both of the child's maturation and widening environmental stimulation. The skills which a pre-school child acquires through his play may be grouped under three broad headings: motor and manipulative skills, verbal skills and social skills. The stages of a child's progress in gross motor skills from the first lifting of the head, through crawling, walking and running, to skipping, when he enters the infant school, are well documented.[13] The progression is marked by an increasing differentiation of response. It is this differentiation which enables the child, when he is ready, to master and to employ the finer movements involved in the manipulative skills of sorting, buttoning and scribbling. In manipulative skill the feedback of information is crucial to the modification and learning of the finer movements, as with the grosser movements. This means that the child must be able to remember his actions, perceive their results and pattern the actions into a sequence which has discarded ineffective efforts. A child beating rhythmically on a drum has learned an interrelated pattern of skills and is employing a variety of senses to provide him with an input of information in the light of which he adapts his responses. The importance of manipulative skills lies in their ability to open up new aspects of the environment for the child to explore and master:

Tim, 3 years, 11 months. On seeing Tim in a nursery play situation, the observer tried to gauge first how well developed Tim's motor behaviour was. He reached many of the norms of a four year old which Gesell presents in *The First Five Years of Life*. His sitting position was always very upright, he was adept at manipulating small objects, like a straw or a toy railway truck, between thumb and first finger. He seemed to take pleasure in moving furniture, in washing bottles and in handling equipment, and it was apparent that this pleasure came from confidence. At times he laughed out loud at the success of his movements.

The learning of speech includes the learning of motor skills, the patterning of sound through the movements of the speech organs. It is a complex of skills in which the child employs the sounds to reveal his understanding of his environment and to accommodate to it:

Clair, exactly 4 years, has just chosen a book from the book corner. Richard, 4 years, 3 months, came up and snatched it. Clair defended her property, 'No, no. Stop it. Richard's taken all mine.' Richard drops the book and runs off. Clair opens the book in the middle. 'O yes, O yes,' as she lifted up and lowered her shoulders. 'O yes.' She turned the pages keeping up a constant half-sung commentary. 'Raining, raining,' of a picture showing a storm. 'A-um, a-um,' as she turned the pages. She makes what appears to be disapproval noises at a picture, 'st, st.' She tries to turn a large number of pages together and has difficulty in separating them. She shuts the book and takes another one. She opens the book but without looking carefully at the pages. She sings, 'One day there was a ——.' She looks away looks back and turns the pages. She laughs as the pages flick back and she loses her place. She picks up a third book, says, 'Oo.' She lifts a hand towards Richard. who has come to look, 'Big bull, Richard. Richard, there's a big bull. Tessa there's a big bull, Oo a bear another bear, that's a bear, no.' She shuts the book and gets up to follow Tessa.

Since a child's speech indicates his stage of mental development and the way he interprets the world, his speech will change in the direction of greater reality and precision as his framework of reference grows more realistically based.

A child's increasing skill in language is a reflection of his cognitive development. When a child's speech indicates an attitude such as a refusal to conform to the wishes of another, the responses of others to his words act as a reinforcement to confirm or modify his attitude. He learns in this way to persist in or to adapt the language he uses. When he has reached the point at which playing with others is an inevitable step in his development, the responses of other children act as further modifying influences upon his language; new roles and new functions teach him new forms of expression. In his co-operation with others he learns subtler uses of language in order to influence them.[14]

Language is one of the chief instruments by which children acquire the social skills necessary for successful group play. It underlines the behaviour appropriate to the roles they adopt; it reinforces their forms of cooperation, assertion and submission. It is employed as a substitute for physical persuasion and skill in language affords a legitimate route for the achievement of their ends. Children's play involves quite complex social situations which demand both rules and standards. The acceptance of these has to be learnt by the child as a condition of taking part in group play.

Children of pre-school years move away from the judgment of an act in terms of its reinforcement to the judgment of an act in terms of the rule that applies to it:

Ian, 3 years, 11 months. After washing his hands, Ian walked to the towels which were hung up with pictures on each towel and flannel for identification purposes. Ian had an umbrella on his. He stood and looked at the towels. His eyes travelled slowly round all of them. He walked straight to his and wiped his hands without taking it down. Ian pointed to his label on the towel and said to a nearby watching boy, 'That's one umbrella there,' and pointing to his flannel, 'and there's another.'

Ian seemed to be at the stage when he learnt standards of behaviour from his environment and had begun consciously to apply them to himself and others.

Through play children undertake a range of activities which at their level of development covers every aspect of human activity from the physical to the moral. Play essentially embodies the idea of free choice among these activities and out of these choices their interests develop.

4

Interests, learning and achievement-1

Interests differ from attitudes in that they are directed towards a specific object, person or activity. An interest always implies an attraction towards the object. One might say that interests are a form of favourable attitudes, directed to an object, issuing in behaviour which satisfies a need.[1] The need directs attention to these objects which will satisfy it and out of the active pursuit of these objects interest is developed. This interest has its own psychological characteristics. Its pursuit engages the whole child. His concentrated attention is given to it and he is unaware of both the effort he is putting forth and the time that it is taking. It is to be presumed that the child is afforded the widest variety of materials to be interested in before any conclusions can be drawn about the range of his interests. Opportunity is one of the factors which shape interests. The choice may be influenced not only by opportunities within the environment, but by the developing powers of the child. Children are unable to acquire interests if the facilities are limited. The first objects of interest to an infant are those which satisfy his physical needs. It is not until he is mobile that he can begin to explore physically the environment which surrounds him. The early interests of a young mobile child are centred on the available materials of his physical environment, and his ability to progress from these depends upon his maturation. As the scope of his experiences increases he finds a wider range of objects for his interest. As one need becomes dominant or replaces another so the child's objects of interest change and this gives some indication of his changing needs. Interests at this age are not stable. To exploration and curiosity is allied manipulation and from these beginnings develop interests in manipulative toys and objects, raw materials and toys on wheels:

John, 1 year, 2 months, had been walking for one week. At the time of observation the immediate objects of his attention were a red ball (the size of a tennis ball) and a largish grapefruit. He attempted unsuccessfully to pick up both objects in palm or hand grasps and to walk with them. Three times he was unsuccessful in his efforts. At the fourth attempt he clutched the grapefruit to his chest with his right hand and held the ball in his left palm. With feet wide apart he walked successfully carrying both objects to the other side of the room.

Julian, 3 years, 11 months. His adaptive powers appeared limited. He maintained longest his activity with the train. He developed this play very little in the 25 minutes he was involved in it. It seems possible that he chose this equipment in the first place because it held few creative possibilities; the track was set up and the trucks were provided; all Julian did was to vary the rhythms and speed of locomotion. His movements were repetitive and there was little differentiation in function. The trucks were pushed, pulled and swung indiscriminately.

As a child grows older his interests tend to diverge. The learning of skills develops opportunities for dealing in more ways with established interests and increases their complexity. What at first may be isolated play with a doll, later may be transformed into playing out a complex family situation involving perceptual, motor and social learning. Owing to their greater competence in handling materials, living with other people and understanding their world, the interests of the older are much richer than those of younger pre-school children.

At the same time fantasy interests are developing out of the child's experience of what takes place in the outside world. These experiences demand fuller exploration: they may be appealing, and he wants to repeat them; they may be difficult to understand, and he wants to interpret them; they may have emotional overtones, and he wants to come to terms with them. In his fantasy play the child repeats and recombines his experiences in new forms which satisfy his own needs and help him to interpret the environment in his own way. Fantasy play is flexible, so that the child can invest objects in the outer world with the qualities of his own imaginative life. By recreating through his own behaviour the situations of real life he can accommodate himself to the world.

Deborah, 4 years, 6 months, and Karen, 4 years, 6 months. They have a box of dressing up clothes. Deborah is dressed in a veil and is rummaging in the box, Karen is also wearing a veil. Deborah delves into the box, searching at the back and bottom of it, 'I ain't got three dresses, have I?' Karen sees and picks up a skirt with her right hand, and looks at it, 'What's this dress? Yes, that's for me.' Deborah turns round then says, 'You're not having this. This is a bride's thing.' Two four year old boys boisterously charge into the girls. Deborah pushes one of them firmly and says, 'Get off my feet,' then to the other, who is about to sit on the chair she had been occupying, 'Don't, that's my seat.' Deborah takes the skirt, sits on her chair, puts her feet into the skirt, right foot first; she stands, pulls up the skirt at the front and then tucks in her dress at the back. Karen says, 'I thought you were a bride.' Deborah says, 'I am a bride,' and to the boys, 'We don't want any fights in here.'

Creative interests provide all-absorbing activities for the child. In whatever the medium, the perceptual-motor exploration of the material is followed by manipulative experimentation. When the results of his experimentation link up with the images that he has formed from his experiences, he finds a correspondence between the products of his experimentation and the external world. At this stage he can offer a name for his product. True creativity does not arise until he can first decide what he is going to do before he sets to work. The content of his work is in symbolic form. This means that he represents what he knows and understands about his experiences. and his symbols bear little likeness to the objects of his experience. The symbol for a man, for example, may be a ring with two 'eyes'. As the child's perceptual and motor skills develop, so the detail of his symbols, becomes more differentiated and interrelated. The choice of his symbols and the ways in which he arranges and rearranges them, reflect in his creative interests his preoccupation with his own feelings and interests. Creative activity can employ movement, paints, clay, word and other materials and is more successful if it takes place in the supporting presence of an adult who has offered him a range of materials from which to choose and who keeps them in a workable condition. Each child's product is unique and the criteria of success and failure cannot be applied to it. At the same time children are interested in listening to stories through which some process of identification is possible and out of this, as their own linguistic skill develops, they evolve the creation of their own stories, rhymes, verbal puzzles and other forms of word play.[2]

Sharon, 3 years, 6 months, riding on the indoor roundabout was saying, apparently to herself, 'Ding a ding; ding a dong; ding a dang; ding, dong, dang.'

The importance of creative interests can be shown by the concentration children give to them. Their value lies in the contribution they make to the reduction of children's anxieties by offering them means for satisfaction and success. No interest develops to the exclusion of others. Side by side with creative play, motor and manipulative interests continue and become transformed into constructive and adventure play in which the child passes to more independent forms of achievement.

The child's first responses to the world are characterized by the dependency which arises from his helplessness, the aggression which arises from his existence as a personality, and the anxiety which arises from the conflict between them. He has however, as a human being, been endowed both with a compelling desire to come to terms with external reality and to master it and also with the equipment to attain that mastery. These activating principles of learning do not progress in a straight line of accomplishment but are marked by setbacks at one time and remarkable advances at another. These are determined by the appearance together of the prerequisite skills, gained through experience, and physical and neural maturation. Such skills make a child ready to tackle a new task. Their absence makes the task meaningless to him. They are occasioned by the opportunities or deprivations of the material environment, or by the

33

reinforcement or lack of it provided by the adults surrounding the child.

During the first two years of life the child begins the task of discrimination learning, that is, learning to distinguish between the different properties of different objects and to associate the stimuli he receives from them with the differences. He selects from the many stimuli afforded by the object those which, as cues, indicate its most important characteristics. The occurrence of comparable cues, when a child is presented with them preferably at the same time rather than successively, enables him to make the same response to similar stimuli. This is the process of stimulus generalization. This identity of response is, in sensorimotor terms, the first step towards classification.[3] This capacity for similarity of response establishes patterns of response to the external world which go to form his framework of reference for these objects. New experiences are built into the existing framework. This framework employs a primitive nonverbal form of classification. The recurrent recognition of similar stimuli within a framework of reference leads to repeated similarity of response through which motor habits are established. The development of an interrelationship between perceptual discrimination and regularity of response known as the sensori-motor stage provides a way of organizing the first disparate events in an infant's life:

John, 1 year, 2 months. He splashed vigorously with both arms and legs in his bath at home. When away from home for the first time, and put into a larger bath, he sat quietly and still in it for a few moments. Then supported by his mother's arm, he flexed his body and thrashed his arms and legs in the water. He paused, smiled and repeated the action.

An important development takes place when the child begins to discover that his motor activities can modify his environment by reorganizing items within it. This involves intention. It means that he is beginning to change his framework or accommodate it to new environmental challenges. As he reshapes his motor habits to apply them to new situations he begins to show goal-directed operations. Objects take on permanency and stimulus generalization is reinforced.[4]

The process of modifying responses in the light of goal-directed behaviour is accelerated and transformed by the use of language:

Diane, 4 years, 4 months, finishes tidying one cot and turns her attention to the second bed. Her way is blocked by Peter who is sitting on a stool, 'Excuse me, Peter, but I have to get the clothes.' Peter moves; Diane goes to the cot and starts to tidy it. As she does this she says, 'I've gotta do this properly.' She completes her task, walks briskly out of the Wendy house and sits on a chair ready for a story.

To name an object gives it permanency and confirms those cues by which it is identified. It reinforces discrimination between the cues and lifts the classifying process from the level of consistency of response to consistency of language.[5] The child's language clarifies his concepts and enables him to relate them to each other either horizontally, as when he experiences a range of objects which make up first order concepts such as 'dog' or 'cat'; or vertically, when he can reach towards second order concepts such as 'animal'. At the same time the order of words in a sentence and the structure of language enable him to consolidate relationships between his concepts.[6] He can bring his level of conceptual development into relationship with that used to order the world through the use of the conventions of language:

Alison, 2 years, 7 months, looks at a picture of a girl wearing a blue jumper and black trousers. She points to the jumper, 'What's that? Boo.' She points to the trousers, 'What that? Dark boo.'

This increasing cognitive mastery of the pre-school child is the instrument by which he seeks to attain his goals. These goals are determined by his readiness to tackle them and in the normal development of the child a succession of these provides him with developmental tasks. Such tasks are goals for present striving; success in them is prerequisite experience for success in approaching future developmental tasks. A child who is learning to walk is not only set towards achievement but when he succeeds he has acquired essential experience, required for successful running, jumping or balancing on a bar. The most favourable conditions for success in a developmental task are not only readiness but opportunity, in an environment which reduces chances of failure and provides the reinforcement of approval:

Helen, 3 years, 5 months. She is getting up. She kicks off her own pyjama trousers and sits on the floor. She successfully pulls a sock on to her left foot using thumb and forefinger to grip with both hands. She attempts the right sock but is unsuccessful and says, 'I really can't do it, I've tried twice!' She perseveres and finally succeeds.

She then puts on in turn her left sandal, and right sandal. She realises she is still wearing her pyjama coat, 'Daddy will you do the buttons now?' Father offers help but she pushes his hands away; 'Oh, I have to do them, 'cos I can do them.' She is successful, takes off the coat, drops it on the floor and slides on her vest, 'Have I got it back to front Daddy?' She picks up her tee shirt and slips it on similarly, 'I like this tee shirt. Where's my pants though?' Helen leans back, with her back against the bed, stands on her right leg and puts her left leg in her pants. She then tries to balance on her right leg and fails. She says, 'O, I can't get the 'nother leg on!'

Mother takes them off, straightens them, and she successfully pulls them on at the first attempt. 'There! Now my shorts!' She holds them up in both hands and says, 'Mummy, is this the right way?' She puts her left leg in, then her right, and successfully pulls on her shorts.

Mother says, 'Pick up your pyjamas.'

Helen, 'You have to do Mummy, 'cos I don't know how to do it like that!'

Mother, 'You try.'

Helen, 'Well, I don't want to.' But she picks them up and throws them into her cot. 'I done it,' she says and runs to the bathroom.

The developmental tasks which face the pre-school child in Western society are weaning, walking and talking, bladder and bowel control, dressing, eating, control of anger and aggression, and distinguishing between 'mine' and 'thine', and between 'good' and 'bad' according to the standard of the culture in which he is being brought up.

Different ways of approaching the organization of knowledge and the use of skills required to achieve children's goals begin to emerge. Through their successes these differences are reinforced. Some children select their knowledge from the point of view of its usefulness to the task in hand, some seem to be more interested in seeing the relationships between the elements it possesses and are concerned in organizing it into a satisfying pattern, while others rely much more upon a vivid hold upon past experience and on good memory. These strategies or ways of organizing one's knowledge in order to achieve a goal may occur in certain dimensions at the extremes of which there are those children who take open or closed ways of tackling the problem. Open ways are marked by a constructive, comprehensive, intuitive approach; closed ways by an analytical part-by-part approach.[7] As tasks and problems become more complex and involve greater verbalization so these cognitive styles play a more important part in the child's aproach and method of solving problems. Each child will arrive in his own way at the means of success and the rewards of achievement.

Alison, 2 years, 7 months, is exploring a box from the greengrocers. She takes up some wrapping paper in her hand. 'It's paper.' She puts down the paper and takes up half a cucumber. 'What's that? Coocumber.' She puts down the cucumber and picks it up a second time. 'Yess, that's two coocumbers.' As she handles the remaining oranges in turn she says, 'What's that? An apple.' 'No, that's an orange too.' 'That's an orange too.' 'That's an orange too.' 'That's, what? Coo, that's coocumber.'

The concept of achievement necessarily involves standards of excellence, evaluation, success and failure, and levels of aspiration.[8] The standards of excellence may be external, revealed by the appreciation or depreciation of others, or internal, held by the performer himself. Evaluation is the application of these standards to the work: by these the work is judged to succeed or fail in terms of the standards of excellence. Experience of success or failure leads the performer to set himself a level of aspiration for future performances and to strive for it with persistence. His present effort is related to his future goals. The concept therefore includes not only the drive for achievement but also the varying levels of motivation at which it functions.

The pre-school child has already come to terms with all these features which make for achievement. When he enters school his growth into the middle years of childhood will depend upon the motivation of his achievement and to the attitudes that he is forming towards his tasks, his peers, and those adults, like the teacher, whose function is to help him achieve:

Tim, 3 years, 11 months, on the climbing frames was able to demonstrate his achievement to an adult, using language and the adult's presence to precipitate a difficult action. 'I'm going to jump from here.' Again Tim's skill in manoeuvreing the trolley put him into a position of command, and hence gave him a sense of power, 'I go fast.' His words flowed more fluently; his enjoyment was expressed in loud laughter, he was showing appreciation in acting in the presence of the adult.

One of the most important signs of deviant development is to be found in a child's failure to achieve the goals that are appropriate to his age. The causes of this are as complex as the factors which make for success. They may lie within the child himself, owing to a lack of physical or mental ability. They may be linked with emotional factors which derive from his infant experiences. He may be overdependent or deprived of the chance of developing a true dependency.[9] His aggression or his anxiety may prevent him from playing. His attitudes to others and to authority may be stunted with corresponding difficulties in laying the foundations of a realistic approach to the problems which face him. He will lack fulfilment in his play. All these will hinder his success and limit the opportunities for discovering the joys of achievement.

5

Some implications for the education of the pre-school child

The dependency needs of the infant are the grounds for his first claims upon the adult who is responsible for him. It is assumed that his physical needs are met but since it is impossible to dissociate his physical from his psychological needs, the ways in which they are met are of paramount importance. The mothering of young children demands a natural affectionate response which helps a child to realize his own existence as a person worthy of love. Feeding and bathing may become occasions for the interchange of affection. Nevertheless, since the child has his own instinctual life, outbursts of aggression and anger are inevitable. He should not obtain his purposes through such outbursts, or an undesirable reinforcement will take place. The environment should rather be manipulated by the adult so that he can obtain what he wants in other ways or find a substitute goal. This behaviour will be helped by consistency of parental response to such outbursts. An established routine gives the child a framework of expected behaviour into which he can fit any shattering new experiences.

In the same way when he is a little older and has begun to make social contacts with other children, the presence of the supporting adult, his mother or father, or another child's parent, is necessary to help him deal with the inevitable aggression and anger which will from time to time mark his social experiences.

The first contact that some children will have outside the family will be when they enter the play group or the nursery school. The child's continuing development depends upon the nursery school teacher's awareness of the fact that the nursery school is an extension of and supporting influence to the good home. Her role cannot be that of a mother, though it must supply the children with similar support. This can only come from her respect for each of her children as a person. She is friendly and sincere in her acceptance of each child.

To ensure that the child coming from the intimacy of his family circle is not plunged into a bewilderingly large group of children, he is given other adults in the form of nursery assistants to whom he can turn. The teacher is responsible both for the children and the assistants. In order to complement the children's mothers the teacher must know enough about children's development not to be disturbed by whatever happens. Her calm acceptance of their behaviour will ensure the children's continuing trust in the atmosphere she provides for them. At the same time she needs to know the mothers of her children and their families well enough to appreciate the best ways of continuing the support of a good home and compensating for the effects of a disadvantaged home. When the child sees his mother and teacher in friendly conversation he is reassured, and the presence of his mother in the nursery day by day reinforces his assurance.[1]

The second function of the nursery school teacher is to provide a physical environment which continues and extends the child's exploration of the nature and qualities of things. It will help him to accept the nursery school situation if among the materials and equipment he can recognize toys which have already formed part of his experience at home. Beyond this the nursery teacher has to provide the further materials which will extend his experience. Primitive material like sand, water and clay offer an opportunity for expression and manipulation to children at many different levels of development:

Ian, 3 years, 11 months. Observations of Ian over a period of four weeks revealed that he seemed to have developed confidence in a number of activities. He showed some adaptive ability particularly in the water play which absorbed him fully for ten minutes and in which he worked out by trial and error a system of pouring through a funnel into a bottle. He discarded the wooden toys rapidly because he could find little scope in them for experimentation.

One child may experiment with primitive material and at a later stage use it creatively. Other materials which serve creative purposes are finger and powder paints, paper for tearing, cutting and collage, and junk. The need for constructive play is met by the provision of wooden blocks, boxes, offcuts of wood and dough. Any of the materials provided may be given symbolic meaning in fantasy play. Materials which predispose towards fantasy play can be adopted by the child to his purposes and need not be ready made. A large empty box may serve as a house, a boat, a truck; a piece of cloth may serve as a cloak, a flag or even a doll. Dressing up clothes suggest a variety of roles and functions for them to engage in during their different forms of social play. Puppets provide a useful vehicle for the projection of themselves into a wider range of roles than they have met at first hand. The dramatization of family life helps the child to explore the world he knows and adequate provision for this must be made in a corner set out for family play. Here the children can retire for a time from the presence of the adult and work out the roles of mother, father and baby. They need a wide range of accessories which help their play to mirror the relationships of reality:

Diane, 4 years, 4 months, showed a sustained degree of concentration during the twelve minute period it took to dress the brown doll. In turn she put on its knickers, a green woollen dress, a white cardigan, and a hooded cape. The latter caused difficulty. 'You're going to 'ave it on whether you like it or not!' When she had finished dressing the doll, she put it into the cot carefully, folding the blanket and placing it neatly over the doll.

For children who feel the need for vigorous movement, equipment must be available outside the nursery. Those who engage in adventure play, involving both fantasy and physical activity, require adaptable and life-size equipment. For this purpose they can use such things as large boxes, tyres, a fallen tree, sacks and oil drums, which can be turned to a variety of purposes. Some schools are equipped with more realistic stimuli to fantasy play such as the body of an old car or a small dinghy set in concrete. Other equipment to satisfy the physically active will consist of trucks, tricycles and pedal motorcars which the children can drive, swings and climbing frames. This equipment demands cooperative social relationships in order to exploit it:

Susan, 3 years, 6 months, was adapting a piece of balancing apparatus to make it more interesting. She could not move the big wooden reel under the pole and at the same time continue to hold up the pole. She asked her contemporary, Patricia, for help, 'I'll hold this up when you move it. A bit more.'

The materials provided for manipulative play serve to satisfy important psychological needs for individual children. Such materials are designed to give the child an opportunity of grading, sorting, judging shape and weight. Some children may find satisfaction in using nesting boxes, others in accomplishing a fairly complex jigsaw puzzle. Since manipulative play is usually either solitary or parallel it provides for a child who, concentrating upon the development of his skills, may find solace from the tensions of social play, rest from overstimulation or release from adult pressures. A shy child may turn to manipulative play as a means of observing what is going on about him before he becomes engaged in it:

Clair, exactly 4 years, was seated at a table with a jigsaw puzzle of large simple design. She put in the four pieces, leaving a gap in the centre. Beverley, 4 years, 2 months, on her right leaned over, 'I'll show you where that goes.' Clair watched Beverley complete the puzzle. Clair then broke up the puzzle and started again. She fitted it together successfully, then got up holding it at both edges with thumb on top and fingers beneath. She took it to her teacher who said, 'Good, can you put it back on the shelf?'

She took a second puzzle, sat down at the same place at the table and began to assemble it. It was similar to the first; she completed this quickly and returned it to the shelf. She pulled out a third puzzle, sat down and started to put it together. This time she tried each piece in the spaces until she found the right one. When she finished this successfully she looked up at the other two children calling, 'See, see!'

The rhythm of a child's activities, the alteration of effort and fatigue make it necessary to provide opportunities for quiet withdrawal before further effort takes place. He turns to the book corner, where picture books of information or picture story books or scrapbooks can engage his attention:

Deborah, 4 years, 6 months. She takes *Teddy Bear Coalman* from the book corner. 'I can read it, I can read it, shall I read it?' She opens the book with both hands and holds it, a hand on each side. 'One day Teddy Bear put on his shirt on the door, and the window was open, and knocked the window and shut the curtain so.' She turns over a page. 'He climbed a tree and saw a big horse and a kangaroo and a funny kangaroo. Then he came and he put on a scarf round his little leg. Now when he got in, he got a lovely present and everybody was looking at it then.' She crosses her legs. 'This is the end of the story. Finished.'

He may turn to the collection of objects upon the table in the discovery corner, natural objects or common instruments, like a magnifying glass or a magnet, where his perception is sharpened. The regular replacement of these objects with others will provide a steady source of interest to the children. Other children may turn to the corner which holds some simple homemade musical instruments where they can experiment with the making of sounds and rhythms.

In all these forms of play the experienced teacher can discern the moment at which her own language will help the child to understand more fully what he is engaged in and suggest to him the next step in the process. She provides him with the language which will match and follow his experiences.

The teacher does not simply supply the facilities from which spontaneous individual and group activities arise. She is responsible for seeing that these activities are educative and not destructive of either materials or social relationships.[2] She assumes that the child who is solving his problems successfully and happily does not need her, and she may well show her skill by deciding to do nothing when children are working out their own solutions. By anticipating that stage in the situation in which the children find it impossible to solve their problems, she may intervene by helping the children to understand how to use their materials, how to approach other children, or she may regroup the children by enticing one away, or redirect, by her suggestions, the nature of the activity. It is only through knowing the individual child that she can decide whether a direct glance or hug, talking quietly to the child, a straight appeal, or forbidding, for example, the use of a toy as an aggressive instrument, will be successful. In such ways she helps each individual to learn to deal with his own emotional states by establishing the limits within which activities are acceptable to the child himself or to other people.

This is one aspect of her function of providing a framework in which the children's development can take place. The other aspect is her construction of a rhythmical and structured day. Certain points in the daily programme are fixed as they are in the good home. If a meal is provided it becomes the central event of the day. Coming to school and leaving school are made occasions for personal recognition of each child.

The children begin their day with the free choice of activities, for she has already laid out the materials to attract them. Some will know what they want to do; others will be slower to decide and may spend some time at first in watching others. She knows their absorption in play will eventually lead to fatigue and a reduction in the value of the activities. They will become less creative and less skilful. She has therefore anticipated this by preparing a story or song or musical activity for which they can come together in a group and listen. She does not impose it on all, for some may not yet be tired. She does this when she thinks it necessary and she may, further, respond to the children's request for it. However it arises, this rhythm of effort and relaxation is her response to the children's needs and through it she provides them not with a rigid structure of timed intervals throughout the day, but with a flexible framework for their security.

This conception of the role of the teacher of younger children stems directly from the view that only through careful training and preparation can she make her fullest contribution to the socialization and education of children. Some children of this age will be found in the present nursery schools of local authorities where the head and the teachers have the clearest conception of their purposes. Others will be found in nursery classes attached to infant schools, or in nurseries attached to first schools.[3] Teachers in these schools require a three-year professional preparation. Other children will be found in play groups supervised by adults. These groups have arisen because the need has not been met by the provision of the local authorities. The recommendations of the Plowden Report[4] must be seen in the light of the present shortage which has led to the setting up of play groups.

The expansion of nursery education proposed in the Report means the incorporation of many less well trained adults in the nursery school system. It is envisaged that in a school of sixty children attending full time there would be one trained teacher and six nursery assistants. These assistants will have day-to-day contact with the children; they will be the only adults to know the children at all well and to meet their needs within the limitations of whatever training they may have received. They will be drawn from school leavers learning their craft in nursery groups from other assistants instead of from the teachers. Older women will qualify after one year only. The proposals in effect will place the education of the children in the hands of people whose training will be inadequate to meet the demands of modern nursery education. They may be merely enlightened child-minders. The trained nursery teacher will therefore have to change her role. The Plowden Report suggests that she will be responsible for the physical safety of the children, and seems by default to place the responsibility for an educative environment upon the assistants. She will be responsible for contact with the parents though she will not know the children as well as her assistants. Her role will be supervisory and in this change there is a threat to the quality of the education of younger children which may set back the great advances in the application of knowledge in this field which have taken place during the last half century.

Part 2

The child from five to nine

In spite of the structure of the existing state educational system, which tends to create differences of approach to children of infant and junior school age, the period from five to nine years in a child's life possesses a unity. His developing social and intellectual powers are marked by certain common characteristics. He continues to move from a state of greater dependency towards one of independence through his achievements, but he still depends greatly upon his adults for the conditions of success. The maturation of his physical and mental powers leads him to more objective thinking. He is not yet, however, free of the influence which fantasy still exercises over his explanations of the world around him, and so he is not yet fully capable of that internalized logical thinking which is the mark of intellectual independence. His own maturation tends to enlarge the range of experiences that he can assimilate and accommodate to; this occurs in both his physical and social environments. He grows more skilled in his interactions with an increasing range of adults and children of his own age. His social relationships between these years become more defined and differentiated but they do not undergo fundamental changes in kind. The child of five is entering into those relationships with his peers which he spends the next four years in refining and consolidating. For the individual child it is a period in which his life in school becomes a major influence in his development. He realizes the importance of activities such as language, reading, and, through the learning that takes place in exploring the environment, he comes to meet the beginnings of mathematics and scientific ways of approaching new knowledge. These developments take place in a situation where he can assess his performance against that of his peers. His increasing knowledge of himself is a fundamental element both in his social competence and in his achievement in school.

Children entering school

The statutory beginning of compulsory school education in England brings the child of five years of age into relationship with educational institutions, the schools, through which society seeks to prepare its future citizens. The school introduces him to new forces which play upon his developing personality. He has first to make contacts with teachers who are not only new to him but perform functions and hold attitudes towards him which extend beyond those of his parents and relations. Once the teacher has entered his world she becomes an inalienable and unavoidable part of it. Second, he is more likely than not to find himself in a large group of other boys and girls, some from permissive, some from autocratic and some from indulgent homes. Many boys and girls have responsible parents who have made use of the welfare services and this has given them the wider experiences of regular visits to the clinic, meeting the doctor, the nurse and the health visitor; others have not. Some are fluent speakers using sentences with twelve or more words which they can combine in complex forms for sustained periods. Some at the other extreme may use sentences of shorter length, with words which they employ in simpler forms in conjunction with gesture and expression to convey a limited range of emotional and cognitive communication.[1] To each newcomer to the reception class in the infant school, the other children appear, at first, an undifferentiated conglomeration. The relationships which these children make with each other provide a social matrix in which each child is inevitably embedded. Third, the newcomer spends at present five hours a day in the school, a building primarily designed for the socialization and instruction of himself and others. These three, the teacher, other children and buildings provide him with what might be a sudden and overwhelming range of experiences as he enters the reception class of an infant school.

The reception class occupies a crucial position in the introduction of the child to the world of school. His adjustment in the reception class will lay the foundations for successful learning during the primary school years. His experience until now has been chiefly confined to emotionally charged relationships within the family. His teacher has to divide her attention among thirty or forty children. Her role is that of a supporting protective figure. She welcomes him for his own sake and plans for his activities. She sets standards for his behaviour, for it is her function to mediate the values of society to his level of understanding.[2]

The new entrant has therefore to establish a different relationship with his teacher from that he had with his mother. If his parents have provided him with a structure of expected behaviour at home, he will more quickly learn the expectations that his teacher will make of him. If on the other hand a child has learned at home how to persuade his mother to accede to his demands because her treatment of him has been inconsistent, he is likely to find the adjustment to his teacher's expectations the more difficult. These difficulties may reveal themselves in a regression to earlier forms of behaviour of distress and attention-seeking. The child's mother has therefore an important part to play in preparing him for the new experience of starting school. She should encourage him to think of school as a desirable new experience, talk to him positively about what he will do there, and take him to school with her when she meets the teachers before he enters the school. This initial contact between teachers and parents has been extended in some schools where incoming children and their mothers spend half-days in the school well before the time of full-time attendance. Some mothers have a natural anxiety about this moment in their children's lives. They worry because their children may encounter such things as infectious diseases and bad language. Other mothers cannot face with equanimity the separation from their children. These anxieties are easily communicated to the child and prevent him from settling comfortably into school life. The school's formal organization may contribute to the solution of such problems by allowing for a staggered entry by which small groups are admitted in succession.[3] This enables the stability of those already in the class to help the successive groups of newcomers. It helps, too, if children can benefit from the security of possessing their own peg, their own place at table and, if possible, a corner or box for their own personal belongings. Toys and objects brought from home tend to link the old experiences with the new.

The initial adjustment of a child to the beginnings of his school life absorbs all his energies whether his transition is unmarked by difficulties or whether it is accompanied by stress. Until he has sufficiently come to terms with his new environment, he cannot attend effectively to the opportunities for new social relationships with other children that school provides. Some children of five years will have had the experience of a nursery school in which they have gained the satisfaction of co-operative play in a stable situation with children they know. Others will have gained opportunities to develop their social skills in a large family or with many playmates in the streets and playgrounds. There are still those who will have lacked these advantages. For them a part-time introduction to school could be achieved through the extension of nursery education. Some of them, as in the following example, will not have progressed beyond the stage of dependency upon their mothers:

Rosa, 5 years, 7 months, started school as a late entrant in the middle of the summer term. During her first day at school she was completely withdrawn, cried all day, did not cooperate or even take any notice of the other children. She did not respond to any material and seemed entirely isolated from the members of the class and teacher. During the first week she did not speak to the teacher or to any of the children. She just sat alone. By the end of the first week she was watching children move around the classroom. But if anyone spoke to her, she burst into tears.

During the second week Rosa continued to watch the children. She showed a little interest in the activities but made no response to any of the materials nor shared in activities. She cried less. In the playground she wandered aimlessly around, alone. Other children taking notice of her seemed to make her more withdrawn. When Sharon tried to hold her hand, she pulled her hand away. She showed a tendency to tears.

During the third week, when she was given a book by the teacher, she looked at it. She spoke to the teacher for the first time, 'Can I go toilet?' She still showed no response to the other children. She appeared interested in class activities, stories, music and physical education, but did not participate. She shook off Mary who tried to make friends with her.

During the fourth week, after much encouragement from the teacher, she painted a picture. She laughed and played with two girls, chatting to them until she noticed the teacher observing her, then she was quiet. She was beginning to go to the book corner of her own free will, pick up clay, touch bricks. She was showing an interest in her environment, and appeared more confident though still withdrawn from the group.

The impact of meeting from thirty to forty unknown children in the reception class may at first lead the more socially advanced to regress to less active roles than they played in the nursery school. When these children have learnt more about the other children and the new situation, they will quickly re-employ their social skills in their fresh activities. The socially immature will show little difference from the behaviour of the child entering the nursery school at three years. If such a child is going to benefit from the opportunities the primary school will offer him for learning and achievement, he must, during this first year at school, live through a variety of social situations and acquire a range of social skills.

At first then the social contacts of the newcomers will be tentative and exploratory; some time will be spent in watching others and some time in solitary activities. The patterns of socialization which occur in the nursery school will be repeated in the reception class at varying rates according to the previous experience of the children.[4] Contacts will arise between children working with the same materials or sitting next to each other.

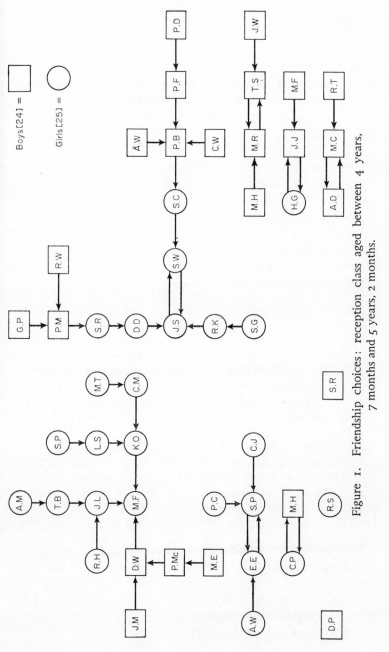

Figure 1. Friendship choices: reception class aged between 4 years, 7 months and 5 years, 2 months.

53

Each child will have a number of such transient contracts which provide him with experiences through which his perception of social situations develops. As his perception becomes more selective, it leads to the beginnings of friendships. Where two friends, however, are working or playing together, favourable attitudes towards their activity ensues. Such friendships are neither permanent nor exclusive but change from one activity to another.

When the dependency needs of the members of the reception class have found satisfaction in their teacher, and they have come to know each other and their physical environment, they are ready to follow their choices of activity. These choices are pursued at different levels of social contact, of which the most complex is the group of children who have come together because of their interest in a particular activity.

A survey of a large reception class of 49 children, 25 girls and 24 boys, aged between 4 years 7 months and 5 years 2 months, showed that the size of play-groups for free choice activities ranged from larger groups of seven and eight children to pairs. There were four children isolated from the group. The size of the group reflected the nature of the activity. The homecorner attracted the largest number, eight children, four boys and four girls; large building blocks, seven boys only; and the dressing up box five, three boys and two girls; the shop five, two boys and three girls. Of the four groups of three, all were girls engaged in crayon drawing, painting, playing with a doll, its pram and its cot. Of the four pairs one girl and boy were doing jigsaw puzzles; two pairs of boys were using clay, and a pair of girls played with sand. Three children played alone, one in the number corner, one in the book corner and one in the music corner. There was one child who spent her time watching the others. (Figs. 1 and 2)

This report reveals not only the levels of social organization among these children for specific activities but also marks the beginning of the recognition of sex differences because only boys chose building blocks and only girls chose doll play. A week later the children were observed during a period of choice of mainly creative and constructional materials.

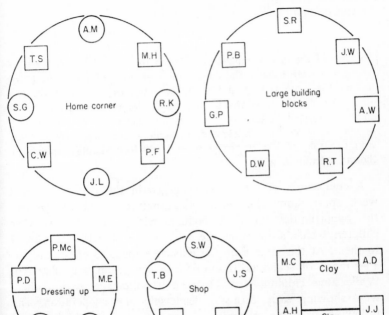

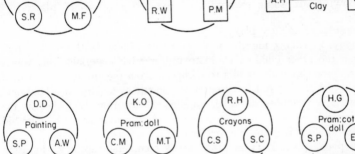

Figure 2. Groups arising from freely-chosen activities: 1. reception class.

The size of the groups ranged from seven to two children. All except one group were mixed. The composition of none of these groups remained the same as that in free choice activities except for the boy and girl pair who used water. Two of the larger groups, one of six children engaged in the house corner and the other of six working in collage, were fully integrated. In some other large groups there were examples of smaller groups whose links formed subgroups within the main group. (Fig. 3)

A comparison of the groups engaged in the two activities a week apart shows the impermanent nature of the groups and the opportunities for close contact with a variety of other children which arose from the wide range of activities offered to them. At the same time the existence together of a considerable range of social skills within the age group was observed. While some children were absorbed in solitary activities others were showing early forms of leadership and cooperation. The following are some examples of the range of social play:

Examples of solitary play

Jeremy, 5 years, 5 months, was again to be found in the book corner when the other children chose to use creative materials. This was a retreat for him enabling him to withdraw from the group, for he would stay there for the full forty minutes, sometimes looking at a book and sometimes watching the other children. He continually looked at the same book and seemed to get as much enjoyment each time as he did when looking at it for the first time.

Stephen, 4 years, 11 months, stayed completely absorbed in using clay, content to feel, squeeze and roll his clay without making any recognizable object.

Paul, 4 years 10 months, went eagerly to the painting corner and, during his painting, was quite oblivious of the others around him. He painted a picture of a house. He then covered the whole sheet of paper with paint. This obliterated his picture and he continued energetically to apply paint until the paper was saturated. Paul said that he had painted his garden.

Examples of parallel play

Susan, 5 years 1 month, and Alison, exactly 5 years, chose the making of papier maché jars because each was anxious to use the materials provided. They had shown no interest in each other before this occasion.

Throughout the period they were fully absorbed in their activity and each only commented to the other on the progress of her own jar.

Melody, 4 years, 11 months, Judith, 4 years, 9 months, and David, 5 years, 1 month, chose clay primarily because it was on the table at which they normally sat. As Melody decided to use clay, the others stayed too. Their activity consisted of tactile experience followed by Melody making a bird's nest, Judith a snake and David a bridge. As they finished, each showed their completed work to the others, who did not attempt to copy it.

Examples of cooperative play

Martin, 5 years, 2 months, Robert, 4 years, 10 months, and Andrew, 4 years, 11 months. Martin decided he wanted to use printing materials; Robert and Andrew followed him. They used leaves, potatoes and cotton reels to print one large sheet of sugar paper. Once they had begun, they worked independently and each boy became wholly absorbed. Robert finished first but waited until Martin and Andrew had finished before they went to play with the bricks at Martin's suggestion.

Alan, 5 years, 1 month, Gary, 5 years, 2 months, and James, 4 years, 11 months, played with the larger bricks for about half an hour, spending the remaining ten minutes in putting them away. They worked as a team. Two boys handed the bricks to Alan who piled them on top of one another as high as he could reach. The three then upset the building so that the bricks crashed to the floor. Gary and James then picked them up while Alan began to rebuild the pile. They repeated this pattern without variation.

Elizabeth, 4 years 11 months, Sheelagh, exactly 5 years, Pauline 4 years, 10 months, and Carole, 4 years, 1 month. Elizabeth decided that their activities with the dressing up box would take the form of a queen, fairies and a witch. She chose the role of queen, told Sheelagh and Pauline to be fairies and Carole to be the witch. Carole objected and Elizabeth replied, 'If you don't then you can't play with us.' They played for about half an hour and emptied the box. Elizabeth directed the others to fold the clothes carefully and replace them.

Common to all the activities of children of infant years is the opportunity that they provide for learning. The quality of the learning may be limited when a solitary child finds the mere repetition of already learned skills a comfort to him. Solitary play is more productive when it is marked by concentration and

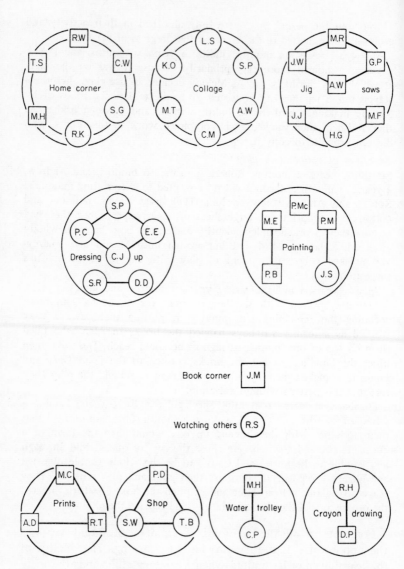

Figure 3. Groups arising from freely-chosen activities: II. reception class.

the consolidation of skills. This is essentially an individual activity. A growing awareness of other children in parallel play provides him with opportunities to modify his learning by taking advantage of their use of the materials in close proximity to himself. To see others engaged in a similar activity reinforces its desirability and associates with it the security that comes from others doing it.

Although further cognitive development best occurs in a group situation it does not follow that children within a group are necessarily engaged in productive learning. They may have come together primarily to satisfy their emotional needs, as in the following example:

Heather, 5 years, 1 month, John, 4 years, 8 months and Melvin, 4 years, 7 months, always played together. Heather and John sat next to one another and whenever possible Melvin joined them. John was an unhappy child and whenever he cried to go home Melvin cried too. When Heather was away both John and Melvin cried. They spent much of their time walking around the classroom hand in hand.

Until such a group has satisfied the emotional needs of its members, which may take a long time, productive learning will be hindered among them. As children begin to show signs of cooperation and their groups develop a structure, so the opportunities for learning for each individual are enriched. The group pursuing a common activity has a cohesive force which directs its members towards modifications of behaviour and new learning to ensure the continuation of the activity. Cooperation leads to more specialized behaviour among individual children which contributes to greater success in the achievement of their pursuits. This reinforces known skills and introduces them to new ones. At the same time the more ambitious nature of the activities which are open to them through cooperation presents problems which demand a flow of suggestions and ways of testing them.

Children with ideas which make the activity worthwhile are generally to be found among those more verbally advanced. This may predispose the others to regard them with approval, and to listen to their suggestions. Others carry out the suggestions put forward in the group. These indicate the beginnings of an important effect of group activities upon the individual. Each child begins to learn the satisfactions of taking a range of different parts. Whatever the part may be it is likely to be determined for him by the interplay of a variety of forces. If his suggestions have been received seriously at home he will be predisposed to making them among his peers. Others from a more restricted home may well be less confident in offering ideas. The already differentiated levels of language development will also influence the confidence with which children approve and condemn each other's actions and exercise persuasion on each other within the group.

Roles and the development of attitudes - I

Children's interactions with each other extend the beginnings of role behaviour originating in the family. They are further extended when children enter school. Each infant and junior school embodies its purposes and values in the expectations which the teachers make of their pupils. Teachers' responses of approval or disapproval consistently exercised according to the norms of the school provide a selective mechanism which reinforces desirable behaviour. This takes place not only with individual pupils but also when all the children are organized in a class group in such activities as story, music and movement. Children at the age of five bring to the teacher of the reception class those attitudes to authority already formed at home. The fundamental task of the teacher of the reception class is to effect a transfer from that variety of attitudes to one of acceptance of her authority. After they have settled in the reception class, which includes the process of identification with the teacher, children between the ages of five and seven years come to accept the situation of being at school.

Most schools take further steps to strengthen the socialization of children. The structure provided by simple rules which make sense to them and a morning assembly imaginatively treated help to this end; above all the personality of the head and her capacity for wise leadership is probably the most important factor in influencing the particular ethos of a school. By the time the child is seven he has a much greater appreciation of what is expected of him than when he entered school. This susceptibility to the process of socialization continues in like manner for the next year or so. By nine years a child is aware of the values of school and able to identify himself with them.

Each child interprets the role of pupil in individual ways. He is not only a member of a class but he is also a member of a series of informal groups. At five and six years he tends to play dominant or submissive parts as he moves through the sequence of his play. Neither a child's own interests nor the structure of the small loose groups in which he plays are yet sufficiently crystallized for it to be said that he has achieved role consistency. As he finds opportunities for experiment so he may tend to play one role or another more frequently. As he grows older he perceives differences in the behaviour of his peers. He extends his social perception, applies his intelligence to dealing with these varying forms of behaviour as they affect him and acquires suitable responses.[1] By the time he is nine years old he can discriminate between differing forms of complex social behaviour and play equally complex roles in relation to them.[2]

Among the many roles that of leadership is one of the most intricate that a child can learn to play. The combination of a permissive home, verbal fluency, a desire to do well in school and an acceptance of the school's norms to behave well will offer favourable indications of potential leadership. This role will be generalized from that of the informal group in which a child fulfils the expectations of his peers to the class as a whole in which he also fulfils the expectations of his teacher. As he learns the role of leadership it is assumed that he will be successful in all he does. Her teacher's report on a girl indicates the constellation of qualities of a successful pupil of this age:

Nicola, 8 years, 1 month, was a lively, helpful, sensible girl whose company was frequently sought by other girls in the class. She had one special friend, Elizabeth, and the two of them talked about their doings in a serious way; they did not giggle together nor walk about with their arms around each other as did some of the younger girls. Nicola worked with concentration and with success in her school subjects. She took responsibility confidently; for example, she tidied the library books and offered to supervise the class in order to help the student teacher. If she was occasionally over-enthusiastic she was quick to heed a humorously turned remark of the teacher.

Children can identify the qualities they seek in their leaders:

Neil, 8 years, 10 months, writes about whom he would like for captain:

'I will choose Alan because he is honest and I go round with him. He keeps to the rules and if anybody does not keep to the rules he would throw him out of the team. He will try hard, he will teach the other boys good ways of playing.'

Other children who equally accept the values of the school may find themselves more consistently dominated by the more assertive children. They may still be over-dependent. Their homes may not offer them sufficient opportunity either for independent exploration or for enriching talk. They may not have sufficient ability to contribute quickly to the activities of the group. Other expectancies are made of these children who perform the role of follower; they learn to be loyal and reliable; they carry out group decisions cheerfully and effectively. It would seem that these children are likely to be found among the middle ranges of ability in a class group.

Some of the most important factors affecting the role a child will play may come from the earlier influences of his home life.[3] The more fortunate children will come from homes with a high level of rational verbalization which reinforces the children's exploration of their environment and provides a basis for understanding the rules of the family.[4] In the nursery school children from such families tend to be active, curious and capable of initiating activity. The leaders in children's groups in the infant and later in the junior school often come from among these children. They are marked by a willingness to establish social relationships and a competence in maintaining them:

Nigel, 8 years, 9 months, in the garden one February day invited a visitor to school to share in the nature activities. 'Come and watch. This experiment is fun. When we put this model of the robin on the bird table in January, the other robins came and attacked it. You see it was on their territory. I wonder what is going to happen this time?'

Some homes lack clearly defined restrictions and sanctions; thus there is no consistency of response and therefore no ordered world in which the child can live. Such conditions may arise as an outcome of the parents' temperaments; it may be due to lack of intelligence, or sometimes to poverty and the pressures of a large family. Children from such families are likely to be friendly when they enter the nursery school but they are less likely to transfer this attitude to the situations which involve relations with their peers. They are less able to cope with the rudimentary demands of infant school groups and they may regress to an earlier stage of dependency:

Michael, 7 years, 3 months, was the youngest of three, his older brother and sister being 13 and 15 respectively. His mother let him stay at home if he complained of vague aches and pains. He was much more indulged than his brother or sister. He slept in the parental bedroom until after he had started school. He described 'chasing' as his favourite game, playing it with his older brother and not with a child at school.

Other homes are marked by parental domination and restrictive practices that are not understood by the children. In these may be found a limitation of language, because it is used mainly to provide clues for behavioural responses.[5] The conforming behaviour that authoritarian parents demand of their children is not generalized to peer group situations and these children find difficulty in accepting membership of a group:

David, 9 years, 1 month, in an 'A' class, came from a 'good' home with ambitious parents. Every morning before leaving home his father practised with him his tables, spelling and the story for the day. The teacher found that David's work lacked freshness and gradually fell behind the level of his contemporaries, though he was obviously putting out effort. He was not a member of any informal peer group in his class.

Such children more frequently resist the social pressures of the group and tend to be unfriendly, aggressive or withdrawn.

The relative success or failure of children to adjust to the social and academic claims of the school may well be an index of their preparation at home to accept the predominant values of the school. The contribution of different aspects of the home to children's achievement has been explored more fully in the research commissioned by the Plowden Committee. The variables which go to make the influence of the home have been isolated into two major groups. The circumstances which include the physical amenities, the size of the family, its socio-economic status and the education of the parents are less important than the attitudes of the parents themselves towards education. These attitudes reveal themselves in three forms: in what the Committee calls the literacy of home, its level of conversation and reading; the interest of the parents in the child's progress in school; and their aspirations for their children. The Report concluded that variations in parental attitudes are more influential than those in home circumstances, including socio-economic level, and these in turn are more influential than differences between schools and teachers.[6]

The Plowden Report demonstrated the importance of parental attitudes in children's success in school. The variables which influence success are not necessarily determinants of roles that children will learn to adopt in their relationships with their peers. The school in providing a wide range of activities provides the circumstances that will bring the child into new and varied relationships with other children. A child can take different parts in the informal groups and in the class as a whole. In this way the school can attempt to counterbalance the disadvantages that children may suffer from as a result of the disparity in their homes. The teacher, in paying attention to all her children, especially those who are neither leaders nor aggressive, nor slow learners, can ensure that their social experience may be widened by playing a variety of parts within the class.

Up to about the age of seven years, children demand that their teacher should satisfy their dependency needs. By the time they are two years older they have fully accepted their integration into the class to which they have been assigned. They now make more specific demands upon the teacher. They expect her to be efficient and fair; if she is so, they will welcome the norms of behaviour that she establishes. They will accept her guidance and instruction because they have in general developed the quality of social compliance which varies little with the intelligence or sex of the children.[7] Their behaviour is less frequently marked by aggressive and dominant outbursts.

The children are now playing a positive part, not only in maintaining good pupil–teacher relationships but also in strengthening the identity of the class as a group. It has now become the centre of their social life. This is the setting within which they develop many varieties of informal social groupings. Between the ages of four and seven years the child's social life undergoes a marked change. He moves from membership of the family to an expanding world in which he finds new relationships with his peers. He has begun the process of learning from those of his own age. The influence of peer groups increases as the child grows older and helps him to learn the ways of social adaptation. Peer groups are not formal organizations. They are characterized by greater psychological freedom than that which obtains in the family or the school where the authority and concern of the adult is always present. The child is free to choose his behaviour and find out whether it is acceptable or not. He learns through the peer group what is expected of him by his contemporaries and in his attempts to meet these expectations his behaviour is reinforced or modified. He can also test his achievements against others in a situation where he is not emotionally committed.[8]

By the age of seven years in mixed classes, these peer groups already show a separation between boys and girls.[9] Different patterns of relationships begin to emerge. The boys group themselves more clearly about one or two leaders or stars. The leaders themselves may, in a sociometric situation, choose one another, suggesting that where there is more than one leader there is not likely to be hostility between the groups. The girls tend to a much looser organization of subgroups, each containing three or four girls. Where a popular girl has established a star position there are likely to exist small self-contained groups outside the orbit of her attraction. Most stars, boys or girls, seem to have a fringe of dependents attached to them through chains of varying length. Pairs within both sex groups occur consistently. In both sexes isolated and neglected children stand outside the network of informal relationships occurring within the class (Fig. 4).

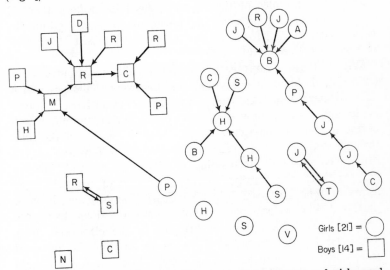

Figure 4. Informal social groupings in a class of boys and girls aged between 6 years, 7 months and 7 years, 8 months.

Children of this age are learning the behaviour associated with their sex roles. The boys' groups are marked by vigorous and competitive activity. Boys tend not to articulate their expression of feeling towards each other. The culture of the girls' groups allows much more demonstration of affection between friends. These differing cultural patterns of affectional, verbal and physical behaviour tend to reinforce the separation of boys' and girls' groups and activities.

There begin also to appear certain links between the informal groups in the classroom and features of the environment outside the classroom. Where the catchment area is large or covers a wider range of homes, the composition of children's groups will be affected by the nature of the area. Children may bring into school the relationships which arise because their friends are close neighbours. Such neighbourhoods will, in a large area, vary in socio-economic status and there may well be the beginnings of social differentiation within the classroom. Where the class as a whole comprises a wide social range, or where a class is marked by extremes of the range, it has been noticed there is a tendency for children of the lower working-class groups to be underchosen and for some of the groups to consist of children of similar socio-economic status.[10]

Within these groups each individual child contributes what he can, finds his own needs met, and discovers challenges which demand new responses from him. The expectations of other adults and children now shape his conception of himself, which begins to acquire some consistency. He grows aware of the roles through which he can satisfy his awakening self-awareness. His teacher is constantly responding to his behaviour and, through her reactions, she conveys to him a picture of one who conforms or rebels, who is bright or slow, who is painstaking or slapdash, who is reliable or not. These reactions form the element of his conception of his role in the classroom. It is reinforced by the attitudes of his peers. Within the informal groups his characteristics begin to mark him out for a certain regularity in the roles he plays. The overchosen and the underchosen are both subject to the other children's tendency to generalize the qualities they possess or they lack. The successful child is expected to achieve well in whatever he does and, because of this expectation, he continues to succeed. The opposite is equally true of the unsuccessful. These roles are not completely crystallized at the age of nine but indications of their appearance are clear. The role of the humorist, for example, is demanded of the boy who has said something funny.

Two processes mark this development. The first is that children's dependency objects which have been widened from the home to the teacher in the infant school are now further extended to include their peers. This normal development may occasionally involve conflicts between the claims of the dependency objects. Children may easily regress from their newly-won freedom to choose their dependency objects among their peers, to an earlier stage of dependency. The child on the fringe of a group may revert to demanding the attention of his teacher or domineering over younger children. The second process is an advance in the child's own social perception. The constant interplay of stimulus and response between the members of his group begin to fall into patterns of cues for his own behaviour. As he becomes aware of what is expected from him, so he establishes a mental set towards the cues which signal these expectations. His perception of himself and of others begin to fall in line with the roles that he is beginning to adopt. In addition to the ascribed familiae and sex roles he is now achieving roles through the interplay of himself and his peers. How other people see him becomes the grounds of what he comes to see himself to be. His social perception is employed in making judgments not only about other people but about himself:

Fiona, 8 years, 3 months, showed three different levels of role identification with her father, with her peers and with older children. (*a*) Her interest in horses led her to take part in gymkhanas and occasionally to win prizes. She identified herself with her interest in animals, she wrote a story about a pony, and helped her father to feed the livestock on the farm. (*b*) She was a keen collector of wild flowers and turned to the more knowledgeable of her peers to help her in identifying them. (*c*) She worked with a group of eleven year old girls at school who were making a puppet theatre. 'My job is to pass the hammer.'

The acquiring of the elements of self-knowledge is not an intellectual process, but a social and emotional one. As a child progresses through the primary school, he comes to know something of his own powers, for his social experience enables him to assess them against the experience of other people. Out of this grows the identification of roles and through an awareness of the differing qualities of others, he comes to appreciate his own. Cooperative activities demand specialization of function and employ the diversity of children's strengths for the pursuit of the common experience of the group. As the child begins to learn what he can do, so he consolidates his self-knowledge and builds his self-esteem. Success in problem solving and the approval of himself and others resulting from this success are important sources of satisfaction and security. They lead him also to expect that his efforts in the future will be successful. At the same time he gradually finds out what he cannot do. He can live with this knowledge because he also has a contribution to make that no one else can do for him.

Some children discover early that success is accompanied by the acceptance of their parents and teachers, and they begin to strive to match the expectations of home and school. Such a child is in a position to lay the foundations of what Talcott Parsons refers to as the good pupil role.[11] This is most likely to happen when the child finds that the rational and permissive attitudes of his parents, or their aspirations for him, are paralleled by those of his teacher; he is then set on the road to success in school. The attitudes of teachers, however, can range almost as widely as those of the homes from which their pupils come. An authoritarian teacher, for example, may well fail to provide the reinforcing conditions which a child may require in order to achieve the good pupil role. The teacher reinforces through her words the role-behaviour of her pupils; her comments may help to make the children aware of their own roles as good pupils if she reinforces their 'good' acts, and they accept the teacher's authority if they are intelligent because they can grasp something of the reasons which justify the teacher's behaviour. The pupil's role is the result of the interaction between the values of the teacher and the values of the child's home; where these conflict, the good pupil role becomes more difficult to achieve.

In a variety of ways the child will begin to regard the teacher as a behavioural model. His notion of morality applied to his behaviour is, however, still primitive. He has passed the stage in which an act seems to him good or bad only according to its reinforcement. Now that these acts have verbal labels attached to them, he can transfer the reinforcement to further occurrences of the action. He continues to assess acts, present or future, in terms of the punishments that will accrue. Both labels and punishments for acts are given by parents and teachers and if the child accepts their authority he can also accept the heteronomous nature of his own morality.[12] The nature of children's moral responses was revealed in an experimental situation :

Twelve seven-year-old children were presented with a picture showing two children of their own age on a seat in a park eating chocolates. They were told that a third child snatched the chocolates from them and threw them into the pond. They were then asked for their responses to this situation.

All the children were aware of the antisocial nature of the act. The less able of them were concerned with the need for retributive punishment, 'I'd punch him.' Most of them, however, showed a tendency to avoid the conflict, 'I'd have caught the chocolates before they fell into the pond.' 'They shouldn't have let him come into the park.' The more able children referred the problem to authority in the form of mother, father, aunt or the park-keeper.

For many children the good pupil role is difficult to attain. A number of the reasons for their inadequacy stem from anxiety. Three elements in the child's world of school with which he has to come to terms are his teacher, his peers and the learning situation. Some children may bring to any of these experiences a general feeling of anxiety. Such generalized states are normally the result of damaging experiences, often in the home. Of these the most important is the deprivation of affectional ties, occasioned in extreme cases by separation from the mother. Deprivation may be severe in the case of children without parents who have been received into child care at an early age, or mild, which may take the form, for example, of either child or parent going into hospital for only a few days. Temporary separation is not only anxiety-producing, but depresses a child's achievement in such complex language skills as comprehension in reading. If a child is in an anxious state the further stresses of learning in school will themselves intensify his anxiety.[13]

A further cause of anxiety may be found in the high expectations that some parents make of their children in the new situation at school. These are highlighted when the child is first brought by the school to reading. The parental expectancies are now focused upon one function of the school. It exists in their view primarily to teach their children quickly to read well. Such parents may show their anxiety in a number of ways: by visiting the school frequently; by making comparisons between the progress of their own and other children; by attempting to reinforce the work of the school by buying the school reading schemes in order to encourage the children to work at home. They know the relative success of schools in the neighbourhood and they know the way in which the educational system works. They have been known to desire promotions and transfers for their child regardless of the teacher's knowledge of whether he is ready for them or not.

Seriously anxious children, whatever the cause of their anxiety may be, the frustrated dependency needs of the deprived, or the over-controlled impulses associated with high expectations, are more concerned with taking steps to reduce the feelings of anxiety than with the objective situations, social and cognitive, presented by their environment. Moderate levels of anxiety may be contained within the social situation of the child, and indeed contribute to heightened skill and the achievement of higher levels of success in school. Considerable anxiety, however, leads a child to be cautious or unduly active in his behaviour, and he may be much given to fantasy. It has been found that such anxiety in a child leads him to adopt a self-deprecatory attitude. This will extend to every aspect of his personality and include his own picture of his physical abilities. An anxious child may fail to make adequate social relationships with his peers. His behaviour may be overtly aggressive or disruptive, or he may withdraw himself from contact with others. The defences children make against the expression of their aggressive impulses, especially if these defences result from overstrict socialization, or external reinforcements like religion, may themselves be causes of anxiety. The underlying conflict tends to be more marked among boys than girls. Anxiety helps learning when the work is mechanical but it interferes with learning of a more complex kind, such as that involving and dealing with problems of reading and writing. In the same way gross anxiety inhibits children's effective performance in speech, language and the power to think conceptually and to verbalize.[14]

All children of this age have some experience of states of anxiety. They can find the opportunity for anxiety reducing situations among the informal groups to which they belong. This is possible because every child of this age has open to him the likelihood of taking part in groups of different age and social complexity. It has already been indicated that deprivation, one of the causes of anxiety, seems to have less effect upon the social development of children than upon their intellectual development, particularly in language.[15]

Dennis, 8 years, 4 months, had been taken into care at the age of 6, since which time his parents and family had not communicated with him. In due course he seemed to settle fairly well to his new primary school; he accepted and was accepted by his contemporaries. He became a member of a remedial class for although he showed a certain lively response to mathematics, he had difficulty with reading, achieving in this at the level of a six-year-old. Similar difficulty was shown with writing.

In the normal school organization the child whose anxiety reveals itself in intellectual deficiencies cannot regress to simpler, anxiety-reducing forms of learning and at the same time maintain the progress which is expected of him. Anxiety is usually revealed in school through its negative effects on intellectual performance. It also spreads from one field of activity to another, and a state of increasing anxiety affects the child's attitude to himself. It creates apprehension and weakens his confidence in his own powers.

Interests, learning and achievement-2

Interests

By the time the child has reached nine years of age he is well launched into the social complexities and intellectual stimulation of school life. His peer groups and his school class are a continual source of involvement. His social interests are important in their own right. His membership of peer groups not only satisfies his interest in other children, but it provides him with a situation in which he can experiment with social relationships. For him, the peer group exists in order to extend the range of his activities; they may be games or pursuits in which the expectations of his friends provide him with the motivation for acquiring new skills or reinforcing old ones; they may be activities which depend upon the cooperation of the members of the group to ensure the satisfaction of achievement.

This pursuit of firsthand experience in and out of school can be conveniently classified into five major categories: physical activities; discovery activities; creative and constructive pursuits and other forms of aesthetic activity; language activities; simple table games involving the following of rules.[1] Physical activities involve large-scale body movements and some degree of skill; boys delight in vigorous and chasing games, often within a simple structure of opposed groups. Girls enjoy the practice of acrobatic skills, often in the presence of other girls. Discovery activities are directed towards finding out about the children's own locality and neighbourhood, and, as they meet them, the phenomena of natural history, science and mathematics. The pursuit of these activities depends upon the development of powers of observation, collecting and classification, ability in reading and writing and, in some cases, mathematical skills. At this age the children's need for extended experience blurs the edges between one set of interests and another. Creative activities are concerned with the child's exploration of his world in terms of feeling, pattern and colour. Through these he increases the sensitivity of his responses. He paints, crayons, prints and uses collage. The use of constructive materials may be employed in two ways: for their own sake, like clay; or as contributing to the realization of an idea, like junk. He experiments with rhythm and melody through his voice and with simple instruments. Language activities are concerned with speech, acting, listening to stories, reading and writing. As their own mastery of language increases so by nine years of age children show a greater interest in activities to which language is central. At the same time the contribution of radio and television to their language development becomes important. Most children are interested in playing simple table games by the age of nine years. These, like card games or draughts, involve rule-following in a social situation. Such games provide a structure for children's relationships with each other and indicate an increasing awareness of the moral implications of these relationships.

It is important to remember that any particular activity may interrelate interests across the suggested categories. Language is involved not only in discovery pursuits but, since it is a regulator of both perception and behaviour, it plays its part in organizing every form of activity. The increase in the importance of language pursuits reflects in part the weight given to these activities in the home, such as the amount of discussion about daily events that take place, the level of literacy required for the father's occupation and in particular the mother's concern with the child's mastery of reading.

The consideration of the interests of children in general terms conceals the sex cleavage in their social life that appears in the years between seven and nine. This cleavage not only implies that boys and girls are expected to adopt different roles in society but also that these roles will involve them in different interests. The generalization that boys are becoming interested in things and girls are becoming interested in people is well known. The cultural determinants of these differing interests lie in our society's conception of the small girl preparing to be the mother of a family, bringing up her own children in her turn, and of the small boy preparing to go out into the world to do a man's job. These pressures make it difficult for boys who show a preference for sewing and puppet dolls, or girls for football and carpentry to continue their interests without interference from both adults and their peers.

That the different social settings of home and school act to reinforce the strength of the growing interests of young junior school children may be illustrated from observations made in a mixed class of 24 eight- to nine-year-old children. They were drawn from a wide range of socio-economic backgrounds and levels of ability. All but two of these children were interested in drawing, painting, papier maché work and collage; a third of them continued these interests at home. A third of the children were interested in physical activities in school, such as country dancing and games. Their out of school physical activities ranged considerably according to the opportunities their homes were able to provide for them. Bicycle riding was popular with both boys and girls; girls rode horses and a considerable number of boys took pleasure in football and cricket. Watching television was expectedly popular; the boys specified a preference for westerns, an indication of their interests in dramatic action. Some girls engaged in such fantasy play as schools or being witches. An examination of these same children's dislikes in school showed that one third of the class held an unfavourable attitude to 'arithmetic' in terms of 'tests', 'tables', 'sums' and cuisenaire apparatus. These children have reached a point at which they have to accept their success and failure in the subject. Their attitude is reinforced as they measure themselves against the performance of other children in the class. Some of the girls disliked 'doing jobs', for example housework, drying dishes, making their own beds and running errands. Already their future life as home makers has impinged upon the life of the girls. Some, though fewer, boys were expected to help in the home. It appeared that these boys and girls were not yet ready even for the responsibilities of personal care; some of them objected to bathing and brushing their hair or looking after their own property, like cleaning a bicycle. The social responses of these children were not developed sufficiently for them to accept the demands that their parents made of them.

The range and persistence of a child's interests indicate more about his social and emotional needs than his intellectual abilities. The initiation of an interest does not indicate the success with which he might follow it, but interests provide the opportunity necessary for the voluntary acceptance of effort and perseverance that enable him to discover the conditions of success. His effort reinforces the strength of his interest and through it he teaches himself how to learn.[2] His level of achievement is also determined by his level of intellectual development. As he becomes more able to perform more difficult operations, so the range of an interest will increase in scope and complexity. It is during the period from five to nine years of age that the first opportunities occur for children to explore a range of interests which may develop later into social, scientific or theoretical pursuits.

Intellectual development

Between the years of five and nine a crucial change occurs in the mental development of the child. When the child enters the infant school he is already capable of symbolizing in language his relatively simple generalizations of experience. These generalizations are based upon the direct acceptance of what he perceives. In his attempts to manipulate reality he engages in a series of trial and error activities. Although he can represent the external world through verbal symbols he cannot order a series of relationships between the symbols that correspond to the relationships between the real things. His language makes no clear separation between his own motives and feelings and the objects of the real world. The ball rolling away from him down the slope does so because it is naughty. This is the period when the knowledge of his own feelings, and indeed, the workings of his fantasy, provides a coherent and adequate explanation for the occurences of the world outside him. He interprets the phenomena of reality intuitively.

Some children, in fact, may have already made the great step forward in understanding which follows the intuitive stage. Such a child is now capable of taking the information provided by his experiences of the real world and internalizing them in his mind. There he can organize them, manipulate them and use them in solving his problems. The means by which he does this consist of operations: these are certain types of action which he carries out directly through manipulating the objects before him or the symbols that represent the things and their relations in his mind. Different operations in the same problem situation are shown in this example:

A group of seven-year-old children were asked how much was contained in nine piles of pennies arranged in a series of piles from one to nine. The piles were counted out and placed in front of them. The less able children picked up each penny in each pile in turn and counted them. The more able children did the same but rearranged the pennies in piles of twelve as they went along and counted those that were over. They were also more successful in finding the correct answer.

One of these operations has already been fairly well established during the pre-school period, that of conservation or the appreciation of the continuing identity of objects and qualities regardless of varying perceptual and temporal experiences of them. The developing operations include seriation, the ordering of things in their sizes; classification, the ordering of things according to their common characteristics; and reversibility, retracing the steps of an operation back to its starting point. These operations enable the child to establish the objects in his world in relationship to each other. The explanation of events can now be given in terms of concrete reality and no longer in terms of the child's own wishes and feelings. These operations lay the foundations for an understanding of physical change.[3]

The transition from the intuitive to the concrete operational stage will be earlier or later according to the abilities and readiness of individual children. For some enter the infant school able to undertake operations which others, at the time they leave the infant school, are not ready for. The transition period may be short. On the other hand a long period may be occupied by a stage in which the child alternately moves towards the new operations and regresses to the intuitive stage before achieving the mastery of concrete operations. This is not to suggest that it becomes the dominant mode of thinking.

The identification of the intuitive and concrete operational stages in children's thinking is made possible by observing the speech responses of children when they are presented with situations designed to reveal the mental processes they employ in tackling them. The language of children following the pre-school years is, however, not only a reflection of their thinking; it is a positive agent in influencing their thinking and modifying their behaviour. They are now able to use words which embody the essential features of the objects and the world itself becomes the means of distinguishing one class of objects from other classes. It is now a signal to direct their perception to the characteristics of classification.[4]

Nicholas, aged 5 years, 6 months, was wearing a plastic helmet and breastplate in imitation of fourteenth century armour. 'My helmet has a vizor like the Black Prince's who fought at Crecy. Here is a picture of the Black Prince in armour, but his helmet has a plume. Will you make me a plume?'

The word 'helmet' was the symbol for a concept which included a characteristic which his object did not possess.

In the child's experience of language he will meet and employ words involving second order concepts, which are those applying to increasingly broader groups of objects. When he is introduced to the word 'mineral', for example, he is meeting the label for a second order concept which embraces the already known first order concepts, 'chalk' and 'coal'. At this stage of language development the wide vocabularies which some children acquire will contain many words with hazy meanings. There are some children living in the Fens who have first met the words 'mountain' or 'liner' through secondary sources, pictures, reading or conversation. Such words need the reinforcement of later first hand experience before they acquire viable meanings.

Conceptual thought involves not only the acquisition of full or rich concepts but also the establishment of relationships between them. As the child gains experience in the use of the language he begins to discriminate those features of the language which express these relationships. He identifies first the order of words and then the use of such signs as word endings, adverbial conjunctions or relative pronouns. There is evidence that the development of language among children has accelerated during the last twenty years and children achieve their critical point of mastery earlier.[5] The suggestion that television with its combination of visual and auditory stimuli may be responsible for this acceleration, would seem to be an oversimplified explanation in a complex situation marked by many changing variables. The child who is well equipped with language is the more able to collaborate with others in action, to conduct a conversation involving abstractions and even to engage in arguments which involve giving reasons for differing points of view.

The years between eight and nine are of crucial importance in the language development of the human being. By this time the able child from a supporting home will have mastered all the structures of his native language. He can show a capacity for varied relational thinking in the use of complex sentences. He possesses a range of vocabulary derived from his experiences, his language models and his reading. He is fluent and uses his speech confidently in social situations. His language is rational and objective and he can use most of the important conventions determined by the society of which he is a member:

Jeremy, 9 years, 4 months, was attempting a definition of 'science'. 'I think science is possibly everything except religion and opinion.'

On the other hand a child of similar ability from an inadequate home who is less likely to have achieved well in school, may find communication more difficult. He is likely to exploit less advantageously the possible ways of sentence structure. Since his experience is more limited, his models less articulate, and his world one in which gesture and action are more frequently used for communication than words, his vocabulary is less well developed and he is likely to respond less adequately to objective and rational statements; he needs the help of the teacher to interpret his actions:

Christopher, 8 years, 1 month, was describing how he had arranged coloured paper shapes in a pattern. 'I just started putting those in there, then I done the same that side, then I started doing the same in the other place, then that one.'

Teacher: 'So each time you found the shape in one colour you put the shape in the other colour to match it.'

Christopher: 'Yes.'

Reading

The child who has mastered the use of language will also have learned to read. The act of reading is the culmination of a series of developments in perceptual, emotional and social learning fostered or hindered by the influences of his family, his socio-metric status and his school. The gradual acquisition of language has reinforced his ability to discriminate between perceptual stimuli. His capacity to differentiate between the varying responses appropriate to varying cues is sharpened and refined when he can attach verbal labels to the cues and to the responses. This capacity can be developed when children are given, for example, the names of different colours or shapes that they are having to discriminate. It has been found that the difference between 'left' and 'right', not normally discriminated before the age of seven can be learnt at an earlier age before children are faced with reading and need to employ left to right eye movements.[6] It is in an early development of discrimination that children find themselves equipped to deal with the many perceptual problems in reading, such as the differences between 'b' and 'd', and 'p' and 'q'.

The development of discrimination and all its dependent mental processes are not only contributory to success in reading but are themselves, like reading, an outcome of the nurturance the child has received. He will already have discovered that words and letters begin to play an important part in his everyday life. It then becomes a matter of moment to him that he should begin to understand what part these symbols play. A confidence in speech reflects a confident curiosity which extends to his picture books and story books. He has already enjoyed the experience of following stories read and told to him. There is no infallible guide to the appearance of the desire to read; it can only be inferred from his questions and conversation.[7]

The causes of his confidence are to be found primarily in the social relationships that he has already experienced. His success in what he has attempted has taken place with the support of his parents and other members of the family. They have encouraged each step forward. Once he has adjusted happily to school in the reception class and established a secure relationship with his teacher, he is prepared to accept her authority and learn what is expected of him. At the same time his developing confidence in cooperative group activities and his pleasure in being socially acceptable give him a sense of belonging in the total situation in which he can learn to read.

The onset of this critical moment may be delayed for a number of reasons. Some may be found in the individual child; the child with perceptual handicaps; the slow learner who needs much reinforcement; the child who is emotionally dependent, over-anxious or aggressive. Others may be derived from social and cultural influences; a child's language and mental processes may be poorly developed at home and in the street. The informal groups of children within the class may result in a child being isolated, and thereby having less opportunity for finding the contributions that he can make to the activities of a school. His achievements at school may not interest his parents. Other parents may misunderstand what the school is trying to do, and their compulsive demands for signs of his progress may set up a conflict within the child. Such a parent was reported in the following example:

Jean, 5 years, 1 month, was brought to school on her first day by her mother, a somewhat serious graduate. She said in the presence of her daughter, 'Jean is such a big girl. She will soon be able to read now she has come to school and start on all the books there are in the world.'

The existence of so many variables in reading readiness means that children at the age of seven will be at different stages in their reading. About a quarter of them will have very little or no skill in reading, a half of them will read fluently and the remainder will need further teaching to acquire fluency.[8] The age of transition from the infant school to the junior school at seven, accompanied for some children by anxiety about separation from their infant school, implies that the teacher of younger juniors needs to be as much concerned with teaching her children to read as are infant teachers.[9] Some of these children will have passed and others will not yet have reached the critical point which occurs at a reading age of between eight and nine years. Before this point children's reading is based upon the recognition of vocabulary which has already been a part of their language experience. At this point they move into reading less familiar words for which they need some skill in their analysis and synthesis in order to be able to help themselves. This critical point presents little difficulty for able children, but in the progress of slow readers it may be marked by a period during which little or no progress can be seen.[10] These findings, together with those about the level of language development usually attained at eight years, indicate that it is a period of marked importance in language development, particularly in reading. Once a child has passed through this critical period he will not lose his language skills and their consolidation and development to full mastery is assured.

Brian, 8 years, 3 months, learnt to read on mixed methods. After having made some steady progress in reading he began to fall in his achievement. A visiting remedial teacher prescribed and carried out a programme of phonic analysis and synthesis within a context of positive motivation until his reading loss had been made good. Brian was re-established as a good reader among his classmates and continued in his improvement.

That proportion of the children who are reading with fluency have already experienced the success and reinforcement of their achievement. Their progress has strengthened them in the good pupil role, for not only do they attract the approval of the teacher and the parents, but they also strengthen their status among their peers. At the same time they are discovering for themselves the enjoyment that may be obtained from reading. Young fluent readers may from time to time enjoy the repetition of successful reading below the level they have in fact reached. They will read primers they have already mastered. In their choice of books for enjoyment also they are often to be found reading books of a level below that of their reading achievement in school. They are strengthening their confidence, and reinforcing their favourable attitudes towards reading.

As their wider interests are means by which they absorb impressions and experiences before their interests grow more selective, so their reading consists similarly of the absorption of experiences. Their reading will expand over a widely ranging field; it will not in general be concentrated on sustained interests. At this stage there are certain lines of common interest. The more able of the infant school children like reading about animals and moving objects such as trains and engines which provide material more easily grasped by their animistic approach to understanding the world. They are interested in movement analogous to their experience of themselves as moving beings and they can project their feeling into these objects. This is the appeal of *Peter Rabbit* in his little blue trousers, the *Little Red Engine*, *Mike Mulligan and his Steam Shovel*. The increasing popularity of Alison Uttley's 'Grey Rabbit' series, from the age of about seven years, parallels a growing awareness of the nature of cooperative activities between themselves and their peers. Children in the earlier years of the junior school extend their choice of reading to include more realistic stories. They find great satisfaction in myths, legends, folk tales and fairy stories. Magic serves two purposes in their lives. It first gives expression to desires the child may feel, in a world of simple morality where good triumphs over bad. The natural laws which govern the world can be manipulated through the child's identification with the story. Children's heroes are more than lifelike and they enjoy and understand stories about great leaders and saints. They do not possess either the religious concepts or the framework which gives meaning to the adult's interpretation of these stories, but the stories have meaning for them in terms of their own psychological needs.[11] Stories about historical figures satisfy these same needs, for again the child has an inadequate conceptual framework of time and causality into which to set them. His literal minded acceptance of the details of the story is the reflection of the limitation of his own experience and mental development. The second purpose of magic is to test the child's present grasp of experience of the real world through engaging in fantasy activities. For this reason a child will still enjoy nonsense verse as a way of exploring the boundaries of fact and fantasy. Nevertheless, as his interest moves away from books with an animistic treatment of such subjects as animals and machines towards books which convey information about them, so he increasingly uses those operations which help him to understand the real world.

The importance of the widespread reading of comics is that they reflect the same developmental interests shown by children's choices in reading books. They satisfy children's needs for reading at a lower level than their ability would warrant; the material allows for identification in the basic comic or heroic experiences of a naïve morality. It gives the opportunity to set aside the natural or social laws and reverse the customary order of things. Comics have the merit of repeating simple situations in simple language. The pictures are essential to the children's interest in the comic. They act as cues to trigger off an expected pattern of events.

The part played by pictures in arousing children's interest in reading and helping them to select what they want to read cannot be overrated at this stage. Young children choose their books on the basis of the illustrations in them. They prefer them coloured and clear. Pictures stimulate conversation between children and provide an incentive for reading the book. Children will look at books of flowers and birds, questioning

D

and commenting, but not reading for information. They are experimenting in all sorts of ways with the extension of experience provided by books, but reading has not yet become one of their dominant interests. They still need both the encouragement that comes from hearing stories read to them and the confidence that comes from their own practice in the skills of reading.

Creative achievement

The element of fantasy which is incorporated in the play of the pre-school child is essentially an experience for the individual child himself. Even in cooperative play the value of the shared situation, as in family play, lies in the opportunity it provides for each child to develop his particular fantasy roles. He slips naturally from observation of the real world to animistic interpretation of it; nor can these two mental processes be rigidly demarcated in his thought. To the adult who can clearly distinguish between fantasy and reality, and its expression in artistic creation or scientific investigation, this movement of the child's thought may appear either paradoxical or confused. For the child himself it possesses its own coherence, which can be seen in his attempts to express his view of the world through the products of his own creative activity. These products are the result of strong feeling; of a wide range of perceptual experiences, the result of well-developed powers of discrimination; and of the process of assimilating them to a pre-existing framework of experience and imagery which is often unconscious. When the desire and the means to express the reorganization of experience are present a child produces a creative work. The content of his creative work is symbolic, and the symbols and colours are organized in a pattern which reproduces his conception of his world.[12] When he first comes to the infant school the child identifies himself with his product; he is unable to detach himself from it and it does not convey to anyone else what it means to him. As soon as he becomes aware of his activity in the social setting of either the teacher or his peers, an element of communication enters into the product of his imagination. He begins to want to share his picture of the world with others and under this new pressure his symbols move from carrying a merely private to a public meaning. He gradually detaches himself from his product as its content and form become the subject of comment and observation by other people. He has added to experimentation with his media an understanding of how they can be manipulated to convey his feelings and ideas to others.

The creative art involves its own characteristic mental processes. It demands the fluency of free flowing associations to provide a wide range of material as points of departure for the children's operations. Children range in their fluency from a smooth and easy flow to an almost complete inhibition of images and ideas. It also demands flexibility, the awareness of different ways of organizing experience to reach a goal. To be flexible gives freedom from the restrictions of conventional approaches. When fluency and flexibility are present they provide the bases for the third characteristic of creativity, originality.[13] This is the combination of elements from what is already known and experienced into a new and unexpected result. This unique synthesis of the child's feeling, experience, and skill is the child's individual solution to the problem which he has posed himself.

The achievement of children in creative work tends to undergo certain general changes between the ages of five and nine years. The content of work of the younger children in painting or writing tends to employ simple symbols organized in primitive patterns. As they grow older and their fund of experience accumulates, their symbols become more articulated, with a more elaborate and differentiated content. They move only hesitantly towards greater objectivity. Younger children are still identified with people they write about, and they are not aware of any need to describe them. The feelings of the characters are still the feelings of the writer, but the more able and older children whose creative work has been encouraged begin to show some appreciation of other people's identity. At the same time cumulative experience not only of the world but also of the creative media themselves leads the child to develop an individual and personal way of approaching creative problems. The satisfaction he obtains from their solution is one of the most important ways he can have of experiencing success. Since both problem and solution are personal to him creative activity strengthens the individuality of his personal growth.

Four examples of children's writing may be taken to illustrate different and developing ways of responding to experience.

Jasmin, 6 years :
I am Jasmin.
I am 6 years old.
I live in a house.
I have one brother, no sisters.
I have a dog.

The next two examples were stimulated by introducing children to three nonsense words: 'guggulate', 'croracious' and 'smeel'.

Sheila, 7 years :
The three rabbits
Once there lived three rabbits one was a smeel father rabbit, one was croracious and one was an ordinary baby rabbit. They lived in a deep hole in the ground. They only went out at night time.

Mark, 7 years :
The Guggulate Man
Help I was being taken away by a guggulate man. A guggulate man is a giant he tramples over houses without noing it. He calls it smeel. I thought that I mite be eaten up in an hour or to. Soon I caught site of the guggulate castle all though it looked like a prison to me. Suddenly I heard the guggulate man open the door and there stood a croracious wife and lots of dead people.

Terry, 8 years :
> I am a donkey plodding along.
> I've the light of the world
> On my old grey back.
> Not a pull on the mane

> Does this man give me.
> But he sits very still
> And holds the rein.
> I am walking on the people's cloaks.
> They are laying them before me.

The work of Jasmin and Sheila is the crystallization of experience into simple verbal statements. Sheila's use of the word 'croracious' is simply as a substitute for an adjective. Mark's writing is infused with the excitement of his imagination and leads him into more complex sentence structure and conveys feelings rather than information. Terry has chosen to describe the entry into Jerusalem from the standpoint point of the donkey which carried Jesus. He has reached the point at which his response has selected and transformed his experiences through the exercise of high verbal abilities.

Discovery learning

It may seem an artificial distinction to separate certain of the child's activities and give them the name 'discovery activities', when in fact all that he does in physical exploration, in his reading, and in his creative work is directed towards a greater understanding of the world and himself in it. To satisfy his aims he moves from field to field of activity; at one moment he is concerned with the objective qualities of experience, and at another transforming them into material for his imaginative life. Nevertheless certain of his activities will lead him towards an understanding of the nature and relationships which exist in the material objects of his environment, and for this reason these activities may be singled out for consideration.[14]

Central to the understanding of objective relationships in the external world is the child's slow growth towards mathematical concepts and relationships. By the time he enters school, he has already acquired a fund of experience which increases with his ability to manipulate the things around him. He has become aware of space through his own movements; he has discovered the qualities of different shapes and that some fit together; he has learnt the meaning of container; he knows how to match objects in a one-to-one correspondence and to appreciate differences in size. He has also acquired a vocabulary of number words of the kind that are to be found in nursery ryhmes, and in the day-to-day conversation in the home.

Children enter school with a wide variation in their pre-school experience, and the first task of the school is to ensure the continuation of this experience, no longer at random, but directed towards laying the practical foundations of an activity that the children will follow with understanding and pleasure. The mathematical material is chosen from their everyday experience in such a way that they can discover the patterns and relationships within it. At the age of five they have already grasped such relationships as larger or smaller, they are able to group the people and the things they know into sets, for they enjoy sorting. Their membership of the class immediately enlarges the possibilities of material for this purpose and enables the teacher to introduce to them appropriate ways of discussing what they are doing and of representing it in simple pictorial or graphical form.

This stage takes considerable time. Its origins are derived from the child's grasp of seriation. Not only does it involve an understanding of one-to-one correspondence between the objects counted and the symbols representing them, but also the capacity for substituting abstract symbols for the concrete objects and their organization in graphical form. The representations themselves become the focus of further discussion and play directly into the extension of the children's language. The children then devise their own ways of recording the relationships they have observed of size or shape or frequency in the environment of the class. In the infant school the material may be derived from such personal characteristics as heights, birthdays and pets. By nine years they are ready to record such things as temperatures, coin denominations in pocket money distributions, and the hours spent in various activities during their leisure time.

Through practical experience of guessing and checking they

begin to find the appropriate forms of measurement for lengths, heights and distances, area, volume and weight. They meet the relationships between the units of measurement which have been determined by our culture. These give conventional form to the relationships they are exploring and introduce new problems into the recording of their discoveries. Since the establishment of mathematical relationships has to take place within a logical structure and since its applications in everyday life occur within conventionally accepted systems of measurement, it follows that the teacher's role is essential in mediating both the structure of mathematics and its social usages to the understanding of the child.[15]

As the origin of a child's understanding of mathematics is to be found in his interest in the phenomena of the world, so out of the same undifferentiated interest he will begin to lay the foundations of an understanding of the regularities and relationships basic to a scientific understanding. As soon as a child can talk he asks what things are made of, where they come from, how they work and why they perform different functions. He may either turn to an adult for the answer or provide his own animistic explanations. The increasing impact of direct experience shows him that magical and animistic explanations are not sufficient. He tries to answer his questions by looking, manipulating and experimenting. At five years of age, these questions can be formulated in adequate language:

Gregory, 5 years, 5 months, was undertaking Piaget's experiment in the conservation of liquid. He said that of the tall narrow glass and the short wide glass it was the tall narrow glass that contained the more liquid. But the emergence of the next stage of thinking was shown in his question, 'This has more. How did it make that?'

The children consider, and discuss with each other, what puzzles them about what they see. They are ready to explore further and more profitably because they are capable of co-operating with each other in solving the problems aroused by their interest.

Scientific interests will arise directly out of their experiences of such situations as men at work, on the farm or building site, visits to museums or workshops, television programmes and caring for pets and babies. Between five and nine years of age, as firsthand experience increases, so the range and variety of questions will increase. During these years they will have learnt much about how to observe the subject matter of their interests, and their explorations will become more directed by their interests. Their language has been enriched by the formulation of questions, the growing precision of observations and their attempts at explanation. Their comparisons and classifications begin to lay the foundations of the concepts that help them towards understanding the material of their interests. These are assisted by the more guided experience provided by the teacher in the development of their scientific and mathematical concepts.[16] Two such examples of the experimentation of children in the classroom follow:

Melanie, 5 years, was playing with various materials in a sink of water. She poised an iron bar on the surface of the water and released her hold, 'That doesn't float see, there's steel in it.' She took a handful of sticks and held them at the bottom of the water and, releasing her grip, watched them rise to the surface, 'The sticks are floating.' She placed a piece of coke on the surface of the water and watched it absorb the water, 'It nearly goes under.' She then took a piece of coal and watched it sink, 'The coal goes under, it's like a submarine or a fish.' Finally she held the sticks at the bottom of the water and placed the iron bar across them to prevent them from floating.

Stephen, 7 years, was attempting to find how many test-tubes full of water a beaker contained, and how many beakers full a larger measuring jar contained. 'I was trying to find how many of them (beakers) went into there (the measuring jar). One and a half. Fifteen of them (test-tubes) went into there (beaker).'

The children's increasing skill in recording their observations in drawings and writing help to sustain their interest and again may relate directly to the records they are devising for their mathematical experience. They will have learned with their teacher that it is possible to do things which will test their guesses. They enjoy the repetition of experiments which they can conduct and understand; through them they discriminate the true from the false. Even by the age of nine the child himself has not differentiated his interests and his questions into discrete areas of knowledge. He does not distinguish between his questions about animals and plants, about machines and the weather. He discovers that there are ways of getting to know the information which will help him answer his questions. In this sense then, questions which to an older child might be seen primarily as geographical, historical, or scientific, are, to a younger child, no different from any other questions that he might ask.

Nevertheless it would be mistaken to assume that a child's growing interest and understanding of what adults call scientific phenomena can be dissociated from his imaginative life. Not only does inspired guesswork itself play an important part in his interpretation of phenomena, but his mind moves easily from a factual treatment to a creative use of the same material.

D*

9

Some implications for the education of
the child between five and nine years

Young children's first experiences of school enable them to further
the process of coming to terms with themselves as feeling persons in a social setting. A child's dependency needs are met not
only by the succession of teachers with whom he establishes
a new relationship but also by the developing ranges of roles he
can play with his peers. In this social setting he learns to identify
his aggressive acts and discover how to deal with them. His
teacher contributes by reducing his exposure to situations likely
to provoke anger, by trying to offer acceptable outlets for the
aggression, and by ensuring that outbursts of aggression are not
reinforced. A skilful teacher may vary the groupings in the
classroom to minimize the possibility of aggressive behaviour.

If the child has experienced much anxiety at home, this will
affect his school activities and his performance in them. For the
greater part of his two years in the infant school, his activities
absorb him, but when he has started reading and writing and
he finds that others outstrip him, he is likely to become anxious
about his performance in such skills.[1] In the first two years of
the junior school this process of self-evaluation develops further,
not only from what he sees of other children's progress but also
from his parents' comments and his teacher's ratings. This self-
evaluation and accompanying anxiety will be accentuated if the
school is streamed, or a competitive approach is a marked feature
of the work of the classroom. Children cope with their anxieties
in different ways. The supporting home helps the child towards
further achievement in school; the home which sets too high
an expectation of the child is likely to increase his anxiety.

For some children the transfer from infant school to junior school at seven years separates him from a world of school in which he has felt secure. He has to make new identifications with models whose values may differ from those who taught him when he was a child in the infant school. He may face this situation every year as he moves from teacher to teacher through the junior school:

Jill, 8 years, 4 months, had settled happily and was working successfully in her first year junior class. Toward the end of her summer term, however, her attitude to school became less enthusiastic. Her mother noticed that she spoke from time to time somewhat apprehensively about the prospect of having a new class teacher after the holidays. This teacher would not only be her first man teacher, but she saw him as strict and feared that he would employ physical punishment.

The child has also to make new social relationships, sometimes with children whom he has not met before. Until he has accepted his teacher and his peers, and is accepted by them, he may undergo some degree of stress which is likely to depress his levels of achievement.

The child's self-picture at this stage includes his knowledge of his own powers, the picture he forms of himself in comparison with others, and his attitudes to work in school. The elements of this picture have emerged by nine years of age and subsequently grow more stable. If the child's identification with the teacher is favourable he can then accept her appreciation of his strengths and weaknesses. He finds, too, how his performance in school measures against that of other children. Achievement is necessarily related to a child's self-picture, for aims which he sets himself which are unrelated to his powers may lead him either to failure or working below his true capacity.

These developments take place within a formal framework of buildings and of organization, the school. The traditional forms of infant and junior school organization lead to promotion based on age, and this may take into account also the scholastic progress of the children which often conceals the socio-economic differences between the children's families. Here the unit of instruction is the class. Many modern primary school buildings offer linked spaces for different activities, and enable a more flexible organization to develop, such as vertical grouping. This consists of family groups, containing both older and younger children. A study of vertical grouping found that it helped children to adjust to the stresses of admission to school and helped in the socialization of new entrants. It widened the range of social interaction among the children, increased the scope of available roles, and developed better attitudes towards work. Though the children obtained greater emotional security through vertical grouping, the demands it made upon the teacher were considerable.[2] It might well provide opportunities for compensatory social and educational experiences that may be more difficult to supply in classes traditionally organized.

In whatever way a school is organized, children need both masculine and feminine models of behaviour with which to identify. Where men teachers serve on the staffs of traditional primary schools, children move from a close contact with a teacher of one sex to close contact with another. Where vertical grouping is accompanied by group teaching it may be possible for children to identify with a number of different adults of both sexes in group situations. It is of particular importance that the four per cent of children from fatherless homes, revealed by the Plowden Committee's research, should have the opportunity to identify with masculine models.

The provision of an educative environment is the responsibility of the teacher. Children of infant school age need the same kind of materials as children in the nursery school, and for the same reasons. Some who enter the infant school will not have attended a nursery school. Their use of materials in the first year of the infant school will be like that of nursery school children. Others, among whom will be those who come from the nursery school, are more ready to develop elaborated uses for them. Their early attempts at arranging things develop into the ordering of events and properties of objects and the use of language to help in the process. Their further achievement depends upon the mastery of reading when they are ready for it. The teacher has now to structure the learning situation so that the children can make progress in reading.

Most teachers rely on prepared schemes in the teaching of reading. The production of reading schemes for children and the arguments which have raged over their merits seem to be based on the assumption that a formula can be found to enable children to master reading. As each new method or device has fallen short of the claims of its originators, so further schemes are prepared, and the teaching of reading is affected by fashion. In this situation it would seem wise to employ a mixture of methods so that each child can gain from one or other approach the illumination that he needs. Two things however seem clear. Where a school concentrates upon the development of reading skills, and has enthusiastic teachers, the general level of achievement will be higher than where the reading drive is lacking.[3] At the same time children's success in reading will depend upon their opportunities for becoming acquainted with a wide range of books. The variety of their pictorial appeal will encourage younger children to enjoy books. Older children will find their reading is strengthened through its association with their interests and their motivation to succeed in reading will be enhanced. Reading many books of different kinds will provide essential practice, help the transfer of skills to take place and mastery to be achieved.

A second field in which the teacher structures the learning situation is mathematics. Her function in laying the foundations of mathematical thinking is twofold. She has to order her material so that it embodies the concepts and relationships between them that her children are ready to acquire. She provides the children with experiences which have a mathematical content, or she may employ structural apparatus which is devised to convey mathematical relationships. Her second function is to ensure that the children are given essential opportunities to discuss their experience. In solving problems which arise she helps them to understand the mathematical vocabulary they require.[4]

Teachers' differing skills and experience contribute greatly to the different rates of progress and levels of achievement of children in school. Another important variable in success in scholastic achievement is the socio-economic status of the child's home. The six-year-old from upper socio-economic levels, outgoing, attractive and articulate, will enjoy his work at school. Within an infant class it will already be possible to pick out the 'bright' children, who tend to come disproportionately from middle-class homes. When they leave the infant school they move to a junior school in which promotion is by age, and classification is by ability. The bright children, whose self pictures include the good pupil role, move into the 'A' stream which continues to hold a larger proportion of children from middle-class homes. The work proceeds at a fast pace and the gap between the streams widens as the children grow older. The bright child has entered upon a process which guarantees his success. On the other hand the same process is equally disadvantageous for the less able child from home of the lower socio-economic levels over represented in the 'C' stream.[5] The situation is made worse for some of these children by the accident of birth date. Children born in the four months from May to August will have up to two terms' less experience of infant school learning than those born in the months from October to December, and one term less than those born in the four months January to April.[6] If he is in a streamed school, a child is already committed to conditions of education which will have major repercussions on his further education and future life. It would seem that the identification of pupils for streaming in the infant school and in the beginning of the junior school is a doubtful procedure on social grounds. Children in unstreamed classes tend to score more highly on scales of social adjustment and social attitudes.[7] The deterioration of performance among lower working-class children in the lower streams may be thought to outweigh, in human terms, the improvement of middle-class children in the top streams. Teachers who are convinced of the value of unstreamed classes devise new ways of individual, group and class work with their children and they find that the benefits to the class as a whole justify their beliefs.

Just as the teacher of children in the nursery school, so the teacher of children in the unstreamed reception class plans their activities on the same principles and rhythm. In addition, as they reach the stage of readiness for reading so closely interwoven with language work of every kind, the teacher begins to devise more specific blocks of time in preparation for reading. Talking, listening, drawing, writing and the recognition of simple words and phrases will all contribute to reading. At the same time she will provide opportunities for the children to acquire experience out of which their mathematical understanding will grow. The statutory requirement of religious education in the infant school poses different problems. The teacher's purpose is to lay the foundations of attitudes and relationships on which her children can build towards an understanding of religious thinking. The danger exists that she may use material and approaches that fixate their religious development at a primitive level of thought. When this happens children, as they grow older, tend to reject the kind of religion they have met as irrelevant to their lives.[8]

As the children move from the infant to the junior school the range of their interests extends more markedly from the home and school to the street and countryside. Their active exploration brings into the classroom a range of observations and questions where their discussions, looking at books and further questions can help them towards greater understanding. This expanding interest in the immediate environment provides motives for discovery and learning and the teacher makes provision for this. Each day a stretch of time is set aside to ensure that the children have adequate opportunities for practising the skills of reading, writing and mathematics. The children need time for physical activity, for the enjoyment of experiences in music and poetry, and for the creative use of a variety of materials. This is the more important because their increasing physical and intellectual skills enable them to express more clearly their thoughts and feelings.

It is clear that the wide range of activities required to satisfy the intellectual, social and emotional needs of a group of children of this age makes varied demands upon the teacher. She comes to terms with these demands by establishing for herself roles which enable her to keep her ends consistently in view. These roles are diffuse; there are no precise requirements laid down for the actions she takes in her complex relations with and guidance of the children.[9] It is characteristic of primary school teachers that they are concerned for their pupils as individuals and this concern is charged with feeling. The teacher's role with children in the infant school as an organizer of an educative environment may conflict with parents' expectations that she chould concentrate primarily upon the acceleration of their children's literacy and numeracy. In such circumstances she has to develop adequate communication between the school and the home. In her role of socializer, she has to develop in her children new reactions to the supporting adults they meet in school, their teachers, and help them to appreciate the difference between her role and that of the parent. At the same time she has to embody for the children those values which are ultimately derived from society at large. So long as English society uses education as a means of allocating children to courses which lead to their later performance of different functions in society, the teacher will have to accept the role of judge and classifier of her children. It is chiefly due to their concentration on the individual child in his social setting that the teachers of children in infant schools and the younger ranges of the junior schools are able to blend these diffuse and conflicting roles in the function of teaching.

Part 3

The child from nine to thirteen

There is an important enough distinction between adolescence and the period which precedes it to justify the separate treatment of the pre-adolescent period of nine to thirteen years. It is a period of mastery in which children discover not only what they can do, but become aware of themselves doing it. Most of them have acquired the instrumental skills needed for further social and intellectual learning. On the basis of their mastery they pattern their behaviour with each other in peer groups which at this time become a major field of experience in role achievement. They have moved far from the ascribed status with which they entered school to an achieved status amongst friends of their own sex. They learn to balance the claims of their family, their friends and the school. The social life of the children is now concerned with the consolidation of roles within peer groups which possess some elements of structured relationships. It may be regarded as a period of some social stability. During this time their more diffuse exploration of the world around them grows in precision as they pass from mental functioning tied to the concrete world towards the stage at which they are more capable of abstract thinking, a long, slow and uneven process. After it occurs children move at different rates and in different ways towards a more selective and intensive concern with their environment. This is a period of transition so long and so varied that children need consistent guidance through it in order to establish their future intellectual development. This time of comparative social stability and fundamental intellectual development would suggest that the education of children between these years is most appropriately conducted in a middle school which concentrates upon this stage of their growth.

Socialization in the pre-adolescent years

During the first nine years of a child's life the early and necessary stages of socialization, which is the lifelong process of entering and adapting to life in the human group, are normally achieved. The acquisition of symbolic thought and language has enabled him to play a more active part in his interaction with those people who are important to him. After this early social exploration, until the onset of adolescence, his social relationships develop a consistency and stability within which he can extend and particularize his roles. The family still remains a major point of reference during the years of middle and later childhood, satisfying his dependency needs. The school increases in importance as a second point of reference, for as the child grows older, its public assessment of his achievement has greater implications for his picture of himself. Tensions are generated between the home and the school, especially where discrepancies exist between the status and expectations of the family and the ability and achievement of the child in school. The child finds in the peer group a way of coming to terms with these pressures and at times an escape from them.[1]

The more stable nature of peer group life in later childhood allows for the repetition of patterns of behaviour acceptable to the group. The continuance of the group gives time for the growth of an acceptance of its purposes and its members find in each other new objects for identification and imitation. Their dependency needs are satisfied beyond the circle of the family and their teachers. The cohesive nature of the peer group now separates its members clearly from those who do not belong to it. Children appreciate fully the difference between in-groups and out-groups and in order to deal with those whose differences stem from membership of the out-groups, they set up stereotypes of the others. Racial and religious differences for example, unimportant to the younger child, are marked off by the nicknames which older children use for members of other groups and cultures.[2] A peer group is also a place where considerable faulty information is transmitted, and this helps to feed the establishment of stereotypes, reinforced by the traditional verbal content of many of the children's games recorded by the Opies.[3]

Membership of an in-group serves several essential purposes. First it helps to reduce the wide variety of parental variation in children's upbringing. This occurs through the embodiment of some of the assumptions of wider society in the peer group. It removes the arbitrary and often irrational pressures of the family on the child. At the same time it begins to provide a structure for the control of its members' behaviour. They have reached the stage in which they have to meet the commonly-held expectations of the group and reconcile their individual and diverse needs with those expectations. The child develops a pattern of conduct consistent with the group's expectations and a self-concept with which to support that conduct. The common elements in the conduct of all the other members are generalized and accepted by each member. This is what G. H. Mead calls the role of the 'generalized other', when in a particular situation all the members of the group tend to give the same response.[4] The child can now internalize the common rules of conduct of the group. It is through the peer group that the child learns to formulate the rules for following the activities of the group. As they grow towards adolescence children can eventually learn how to change the rules through the common consent of the group.[5] This movement towards moral autonomy can only be accomplished in a peer group situation and through the expectations of peers.

The second function of the peer group in later childhood is to continue and stabilize the learning of sex roles. The culturally determined behaviours implied by the words masculine and feminine, already begun through the process of identification and through the child's upbringing, are now firmly established.

The separation of boys' and girls' peer groups, and the fundamental differences in their structure and activities, drive home to each child what it is expected of masculine or feminine behaviour.

A more generalized way of describing the difference between these behaviours is provided by Talcott Parsons's instrumental and expressive categories of response. Instrumental responses are directed towards the satisfactory achievement of an anticipated goal; they are task and work oriented. Upon a child's instrumental activities he will build his attitudes towards work and towards his economic and political life as an adult. Expressive responses are concerned with emotional adjustment and with relationships with others which are important for the immediate and direct satisfactions which they offer. Expressive activities are concerned with friendship whether as, in middle childhood, between members of the same sex or later on with members of the opposite sex.[6] The concept of these responses has been developed further by subdividing instrumental responses into four types of skill, physical, manual, intellectual and social; and those responses directed towards personal advancement and moral development. Expressive responses have been divided into those concerned with emotional security, or a sense of identity with the group, freedom and self direction and a sense of competence arising from the feeling of being engaged in purposeful activity.[7]

Instrumental and expressive responses are clearly not congruent with masculine and feminine behaviour, for every human being engages in both forms of activity. However, the basic roles of men and women in our society are traditionally derived from an emphasis on the instrumental role for men and the expressive role for women. Although in our changing society many women have undertaken instrumental roles through their involvement in work and careers, and many men have developed more fully their expressive role in the family, the patterns of behaviour in childhood tend to take the traditional forms. In the sex-separated groups of middle and later childhood it is likely that the boys' groups will provide, by their activities and structure, some satisfaction of instrumental needs, and that the girls' relationships will provide some satisfaction of expressive needs.

Up to the age of thirteen a combination of aggressiveness, skill and fair play characterises the leaders of boys' groups.

Peter, 10 years, writes: 'I would choose Alan for captain, because he is very fair and the rules would always be kept. And if we lost the game, he would not be angry. And he is not selfish. He will pass the ball up the team so everybody gets a kick.'

Where there are two leaders with their own subgroups these leaders have usually come to an understanding which enables the group to function successfully as a whole. Under the leader there exists a hierarchical structure within which the members establish their own status. According to their skills or specific abilities they can contribute to the success of the group's activities. The repetition of their behaviour becomes expected. Boys learn that their contribution is appreciated and they develop a concept of their own role within the group. In this way they acquire the social competence appropriate to their status. These are forms of anticipatory socialization for the adult and instrumental world of work. This learning is reinforced by considerable expressive satisfactions of achievement and appreciation of their own competence. The foundations are laid upon which the young make can move forward through adolescence to the heterosexual and occupational roles of adult life.

During the same period of their lives girls' relationships with each other centre less obviously upon one or two leading personalities. Smaller groups allow for closer relationships between girls to be formed. Such subgroups are likely to be detached from each other.[8] The qualities which girls find desirable in each other are related to their growing appreciation of their sex role. They share with boys an admiration for skill and fair play but dislike bossiness.

Sandra, 10 years, 1 month, writes: 'I would choose Margaret as captain because she knows the rules very well. Another reason I would have her is because she is not bossy. She works hard all the time. She can run fast and get a rounder, you must hit the ball hard and then you must risk running. Margaret is good at this.'

The informal peer group of girls provides the conditions for the growth of emotional security and friendship which are components of expressive behaviour. Within this general pattern both boys and girls from manual working-class homes tend to accept a greater degree of overt aggressiveness in their leaders than children from non-manual homes.[9] In general boys want to do things with other boys, and girls want to get to know other girls.

Although it is not difficult to extract generalizations about the composition and function of children's groups, a closer examination of the situations which occur in a variety of schools and neighbourhoods shows considerable variation in the forms and levels of development of peer groups of children of similar ages.[10] In small villages there may not be enough children of one age for certain forms of peer group activity. The eleven-year-old boy, for example, may find it impossible to play football except with boys much older or younger than himself. When he goes to the area secondary school where large numbers of boys enable games to be formally organized, he will be at a disadvantage compared with those boys from junior schools with enough fourth-year children to establish a school football team. In such a village boys and girls of the same age may well continue the mixed groups, established when they were younger, throughout their primary school years. A small number of children in the village, extended families, and propinquity may well hinder or delay the appearance of the sex cleavage which is revealed by the sociometric analysis of peer groups in urban areas.

A second factor which affects the activities of groups of children of similar age is to be found in the climate of the school. In some schools where much group work is done and the children accept responsibility for their work, the sociometric analysis of children's choices of each other may show the separation of boys and girls but in their equally free choice of each other for group work in school they will frequently choose across the sexes.

This intermediate stage, in which the children's choice of

those they would like to sit next to reveals a separation of boys and girls and their free choice of each other for activities in the classroom cuts across the sex differences, may be illustrated by a class of twenty children, ten and eleven years old, in a school in a small market town. The class consisted of a large enough number of peers to allow separation of the sexes and role differentiation to appear among them (Fig. 5). The teacher reported that in the playground the boys played well away from the girls in quite large groups. The leaders of each were those children who had revealed leadership in the classroom. Most of the classroom roles were continued in the playground.

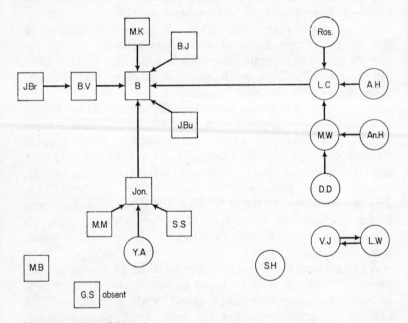

Figure 5. Friendship choices: mixed class 10-11 years.

Within the classroom the teacher recorded the structure and relationships of groups of children engaged in five activities (Fig. 6).

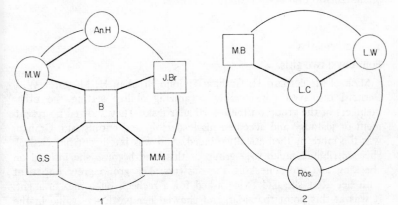

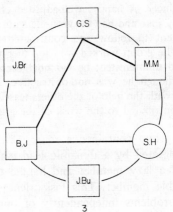

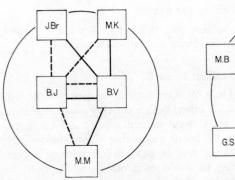

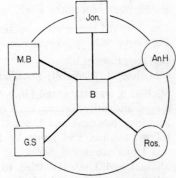

Figure 6. Task-oriented choices: mixed class 10-11 years.

1. Mathematics

Four boys; two girls.

Michael M; Bernard H; Graham S; John Br; Ann H; Margaret W.
Bernard displayed considerable organizing ability setting the other members of the group on their particular tasks. They showed no resentment or jealousy and accepted his leadership and enthusiasm. Graham was the more mathematically-minded. Ann was intelligent but critical. She contributed much to a group of this kind because she insisted on checking and cross-checking the answers. The group grew impatient with her after she had twice asked for a recheck on a measurement. It was at this point that Margaret showed her particular value in the role of tension-reducer. A happy, well-adjusted child, she turned the whole matter into a joke and had the group laughing in a few moments. Michael was content to follow and contributed no more than was required of him. The group worked well together with one exception. John was lazy and uninterested; he did not accept responsibility nor give of his best, though he was not obstructive. Bernard, the leader, was very firm and with the help of the others teased him until he made some effort and contributed to the work of the group.

This cross-sex group contained a range of different and identifiable roles, integrated by a dynamic leadership able to modify the behaviour of a lazy member and handle the irritation of a somewhat inflexible member. This task-orientated group successfully solved its problems independently of outside help.

2. Physical education: work on the box

This involved cooperation because only two people can use it at once. They have to be quick and considerate and move on quickly.

One boy; three girls.

Michael B; Linda W; Rosalind; Linda C.

Michael B, an isolate, and Linda W, were both strong personalities with a deep antipathy towards each other. Both were very good at physical activities. Rosalind and Linda C were naturally quiet and content to follow. Michael and Linda W began quarrelling almost immediately and Linda attempted her usual role of peace-maker without success. Michael and Linda W tried to outdo each other and deprived the other two girls by their rivalry. Michael aggressively pushed Linda W off the box and the teacher had to intervene.

This is a cross-sex group in which personal feelings take precedence over the successful achievement of the task. The group is not powerful enough to resolve its problems and adult interference is necessary to break up the group.

3. *Art: painting a frieze*

Five boys; one girl.

John Br; John Bu; Bobby J; Graham S; Michael M; Susan H.

Graham was the leader of this group; a quietly confident but unassuming boy. He was full of ideas and made the rest enthusiastic. Unlike Bernard in the Mathematics group, Graham could not handle John Br's laziness and so ignored him. Susan was the other problem in that she was depressingly negative, criticizing the colour and arrangement of the frieze. When Bobby tried to make her take a more cooperative approach, he failed because his normal role was that of peacemaker, even humorist, in a rather gentle way. He and Michael were content to be led though they had ideas of their own and only listened to directions as to which part to paint, rather than how to paint it. John Bu. painted away quite happily by himself, engaging in a kind of parallel activity which was his custom. When the main shapes were to be stuck on the frieze, it was Graham and Bobby who finally decided between them where each particular figure should be placed.

This is a cross-sex group where the majority of members are boys. The leader's position was based upon his wealth of ideas rather than on the possession of social skills required to incorporate the two deviant members into the group. It provides an example of the way in which another member of the group, in this case Bobby J, attempted to tackle the problem which the leader had failed in, and the way in which a follower in an ill-led group will sometimes attempt to deal with one of the problems in which the leader has failed.

4. *Model making: a battleship*

Five boys.

John Br; Bobby V; Milton K; Bobby J; Michael M.

Bobby J usually very talkative assumed the leadership of the group. None of them showed any outstanding social competence. Michael and Milton preferred individual work and John Br was usually inactive.

In this group however they seemed to lose their normal roles and worked intensively together. As they became absorbed Bobby J grew uncommunicative and Bobby V replaced him as leader. He produced a flow of ideas which the others adopted. There were no disputes, no criticising, and even no real humour. The moment the work was finished they immediately lost interest in each other and took up individual activities for there were no friendship links between them.

This single-sex group is an outstanding example of the way in which children who have no friendship ties will come together through a common concern with the task they have set themselves. The shift in leadership took place solely in terms of the ideas required for the task and the personal characteristics of the individualistic and lazy children were subordinated to their overriding interest. Like all task-oriented groups it broke up once its work had been completed.

5. Religious education: a play about Moses
Four boys; two girls.
   Michael B; Jonathan; Bernard; Graham S; Rosalind; Ann H.
Bernard was able to use his natural talent for writing and the children chose him as leader almost immediately. Jonathan was an easy actor and brought a sense of calm and reality to the group. Ann contributed knowledge and understanding of the Moses story. Rosalind showed a social empathy; she said that she could really imagine these people as alive, and how she would have felt in their place. Michael B, an isolate and usually aggressive, came into his own as a humorist, adding the touch of bathos and wit which made the play fresh and lively.

In this cross-sex group the needs of the task were matched by the individual differences of the members of the group on which their contribution to the play was based. The aggressive isolate gained recognition because he could offer something that the others could not.

An important element in the relationships described above was the effect of varying need-satisfactions in different work situations upon the children's choice of each other to work together. The teacher reported that when the children were given a free choice of partners for serious or intensive work, they tended to fall into more or less the same groups. These children knew those with whom they worked well and whom they could rely upon to work well. When the children were engaged in freer activities in the classroom or activities in the playground the grouping changed. It was based on friends with whom they could be more relaxed. The children circulated much more flexibly and freely when the end product was not of very great importance. They knew those with whom they could relax best.

One would not expect the children's choices always to lead to a harmonious group or the completion of the task. Their mistakes are an essential part of their socialization.

The consistent appearance of a common pattern of hierarchical structure persists among boys throughout the years of later child-

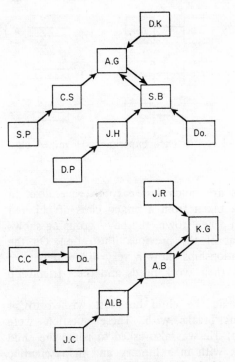

Figure 7. Friendship choices: mixed class 12 years.

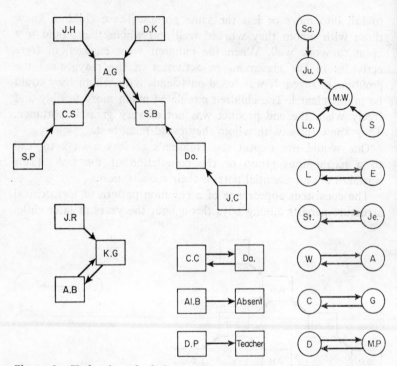

Figure 8. Task-oriented choices: (science experiments): mixed class 12 years.

hood. The girls' patterns are much less easy to generalize. In the following illustration, taken from a mixed class of children of twelve years of age, in a new town, the boys' grouping shows little difference from that of the previous illustration. On the other hand the girls' relationships show a very different pattern of choice to satisfy both their work needs and their friendship needs.

Each child was to name the child he most wished to sit beside and to spend his breaks with. These questions were friendship-oriented (Fig. 7). He was also asked to name the child he most wished to work with in a literary and in a scientific task. These further questions were task-oriented (Fig. 8). The sociograms constructed on the basis of the boys' preferences indicated an unwavering choice of leaders, one of a major and one of a minor group, with only very slight variations in the structures developed around them. The sociograms of the girls preferences displayed rather markedly another feature of the means by which they obtained satisfaction of their needs. This was the pairing off of girls who were old enough to find in another person the possibility of a more permanent relationship over a longer time, to their mutual satisfaction. The members of at least four pairs were sufficient to each other not to want to change their choices in either friendship or work situations in school. Many of these members of pairs reported that they regarded a friend outside the class as of equal importance to

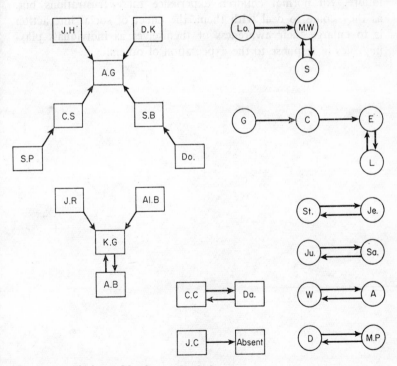

Figure 9. Choices of leader: mixed class 12 years.

their friend in it. Where mutual choices were not totally exclusive there still developed loose groups, from three to five girls, a persistence of the earlier pattern of groupings unrelated to each other (Fig. 9).

Through the variety of forms in which children organize themselves for the satisfaction of their instrumental and expressive needs, they are learning to come to terms with others and at the same time, learning more about themselves. This learning will at times be frustrated. Children will lose friends on whom they have come to rely and in their relations with others will experience personal inadequacies and failures. Such incidents create anxiety. The need to reduce this feeling will lead them on to new relationships or to develop defences against failure. All normal children experience these frustrations but, as they come to deal with them, the effect of social interaction is to enlarge their awareness of themselves as individuals playing roles in response to the expectation of others.

Roles and attitudes - 2

The place which the peer group occupies in the life and activities of children between the ages of nine and thirteen years is so important that it may well be given a disproportionate place in considering the forces which lead to their socialization. Important though the peer group is for role-playing and role-learning, it is only one of the three major systems of reference groups to which a child belongs. The others, his family and his class in school, were established long before he was able to engage in consistent peer group activities.

The family provided the child in his early years with figures for identification and imitation whose qualities he made his own. After nine years of age the range of possible identification figures widens beyond the family and school to include significant people from society itself. Children of eleven years have had a wide enough experience of the media of mass communication to choose for their ideal persons the famous in sport and entertainment or, less frequently, figures from public life. The process of creating an identification figure could be seen in the newspaper and television treatment of Sir Francis Chichester's exploit. The child's admiration was reinforced by the admiration of adults. Many teachers contributed by making Sir Francis's journey a shared experience in the classroom. Children are thus introduced to a range of new personalities. The school curriculum will introduce them to the historical and literary figures of the past. Nevertheless children who are more mature and successful in school tend to choose their ideal persons from among the people they know. They are capable of social and moral judgments upon which to base their choices and can often give reasons for their admiration.[1] The process of identification is thereby more conscious and more articulate; this helps these children to emulate their ideal. The elements of fantasy and wish-fulfilment which predominate in the choices of younger children can still be found in a number of older children. These are frequently to be found among the less able. In so far as their choice of ideal persons tends to be taken from the glamorous images projected by the mass media they are less able to form a reality-based judgment of their ideal persons derived from a face-to-face relationship.

It would be naïve to suggest that this simple distinction between the choice of figures for identification can be explained only by levels of ability. Most children respond to the appeal of popular idols. It is a phase of their development and its duration may well depend upon the satisfaction they obtain from the quality of their contacts with real people.

Ruth, 11 years, reported on this phase in her development: 'Then there came my craze for beat groups. My favourite was Davy Jones. He was very handsome and only 20 years of age. Michael Nesmith or 'Woolhat' as my friends used to call him was my second favourite, he was sweet and kind and also handsome. Peter Tork was next and last of all Micky Doleny.'

These ideal persons serve as reference individuals whose behaviour and qualities children desire to imitate and acquire. Equally strong in their influence are negative reference individuals whom the child knows as those whom he would not want to be like. Such individuals are generally found to be related to the qualities approved or disapproved of within the climate of the child's family.

The reference individuals of middle childhood widen the range of experience of behaviour and values and bring the child into contact with people who embody the norms of a wider society than that of the family or the school. Nevertheless children's reactions to these opportunities vary according to the more fundamental attitudes established earlier in the family. High achievers with an effective self-picture are still to be found more from families where the parents make specific demands of their children and encourage independence.[2] Such children benefit from a wider choice among the values or attitudes which the child can internalize as part of his ideal self.

In addition to the family, the peer group and those persons the child admires, there is a further point of reference for the child. This is the class to which he belongs as a subsystem of the school. This is not the class of children viewed in their friendship groupings, but the class itself as a group pursuing directly the instructional purposes of the school. Through the day-to-day activities under the guidance of the teacher the class comes to accept certain ways of doing things and certain standards of achievement. This can only take place to the extent that the children feel themselves members of, and loyal to, their class, for individual learning takes place in the context of social involvement.[3] What in effect this means is that these standards of work and behaviour determine the expectation the class makes upon its members and the class as a whole provides an important reference group for the children.

There are children in the upper streams who come from homes which fail to provide the aspirations and attitudes to support their children through the formal system of education. These children can often find in the expectations of their class and in their membership of peer groups drawn from the class a compensating influence which encourages them to do well in school. A class, however, is not always identified with high standards of work or desirable forms of behaviour. The poor standards of a class of children in a low stream are in part due to the fact that the children in the class have set low expectations for each other. Their attitudes will be reinforced if their parents lack aspirations for them.[4] So each class develops within the school a subculture of its own based on common information, ways of learning and shared values. In the child's role as a pupil, he internalizes the values of his class's subculture.

The child's social life-space sets him in the centre of a number of different reference groups and individuals. His role as a pupil is simplified in so far as these groups share common values, when the aspirations of school are reinforced by the aspirations of his family, and his friends share them. It is made difficult when the values of his different reference groups conflict. Such is the situation of a child of low ability from a home where parental pressures set too high levels of aspiration for his ability. The role conflicts that arise under these circumstances may militate against the child arriving at the levels of achievement appropriate to him, or they may cause him to become more conscious of these roles, and help him to refine his self-picture.[5]

In later childhood then, the interaction of endowment and the social experiences in the family, peer group and school, are consolidated into individual patterns of behaviour and constellations of attitude. These result from the roles with which he has experimented more informally, and the roles which he has been forced to take in the institutions of school, church, and such organizations as the scouts. As he learns that the role demanded in one group is different from that in another, so he may try to keep his role behaviours separate. He tends to keep the life of school or the peer group separate from his life at home. Parents often find him uncommunicative about experiences at school. Parents and teachers can only catch glimpses of the roles that a child takes with his peers. This need to keep roles separate is illustrated by the popularity in children's reading of stories in which the adults have to be removed, before the group of children can begin their adventures.

While the children are developing the social discrimination which enables them to play different roles with increasing success, they are becoming more aware of consistencies in their own behaviour revealed by the responses of others. One such consistency in attitude was revealed in a teacher's report on a child on three different occasions.

His teacher writes of John B., aged 11 years:

In a task oriented group John was a lazy boy who would not develop responsibility nor give of his best.

In a task oriented group the leader tended to ignore John B. because he could not get him to cooperate.

In an expressive movement group John B. began as usual by being uninterested.

Such consistencies of behaviour and the consistencies of response to them develop side by side with the increase in the role differentiation of the child.

The development of internalized moral norms is the basis of ultimate consistency of behaviour. They become effective when they determine behaviour which conflicts with a child's own impulses and interests and the pressures of external authority. This development depends upon the social experience of a range of role-taking, upon the capacity to look at role behaviour with some objectivity, and upon the growth of the necessary moral concepts of reciprocity, justice and altruism.[6]

An important contributing factor in the child's mastery of these concepts lies in the opportunity he has received at home to discuss rationally those situations in which he is involved with parental authority.[7] The boy who obeys solely because of the relationship between father and son and never understands that reasons can be found for obedience beyond the fact that it is his father who tells him to do things because he is in authority, is unlikely to reach that level of generalized discussion at which the concepts of morality are understood. On the other hand the boy in a more articulate family, where the grounds for the principles underlying the exercise of authority are discussed, is found to develop a capacity for the rational consideration of these problems. It then becomes possible for such a child to generalize from the particular situations of the family to the peer group, to the school, and to the whole social world in which he is engaged.

This in part depends upon the movement from the operations of concrete thought to the capacity for formal or abstract operations of thought which takes place among normal children between the ages of nine and thirteen years. The internalization of social norms among younger children does not necessarily depend on their intellectual development, but full moral development involves the capacity for rational thought.[8] Children who reach the stage of codifying and modifying rules stemming from mutual consent, do so on a basis of their individual social and cognitive development.

This stage of development may be illustrated by the report on the experiment with seven-year-old children mentioned on p. 71. The same picture, showing two children of their own age on a seat in a park eating chocolates, was presented to eleven-year-old children. They were told that a third child snatched the chocolates from them and threw them into the pond. They were then asked for the responses to this situation. The more able children showed little inclination to refer the problem to authority. They showed a confidence in their own ability to find a solution, and a desire to form their own judgments independent of authority. Some indication of this detachment is shown in one response, 'Well, enquire about the child—it's not obvious why he did it—I expect he was jealous—go and see the parents and see why.' A number of responses gave reasons, 'I think they should tell the little boy not to take them without asking, but seeing that he was poor to let him off.' Most of the abler children's responses were stated objectively in the third person.

The less able children still referred to authority, 'Go and tell his mother' and felt the need for retributive punishment.

A comparison of the results of this experiment conducted with able and less able groups of seven and eleven-year-old children suggests strong indications of three ways of thinking. The responses of the less able seven-year-olds are simple, concerned with one aspect of the problem only, to which no real solution, but merely the bare statement of an action, is offered. These are some of the marks of intuitive thought. The more able seven-year-olds and the less able eleven-year-olds tend to respond in a way which is restricted to what their own actions would most likely be within the problem situation. The solutions are feasible but the children are involved in the situation. These are some of the marks of concrete thinking. The more able eleven-year-olds tend to treat the problem with detachment, making assumptions, forming hypotheses and suggesting causes. These provide examples of formal operations or propositional thinking. There is also shown a general increase in sympathetic, and a decrease in retributive responses with both increasing age and greater ability. The tendency to avoid the conflict situation, very marked in the younger children, had almost disappeared in the older children. By eleven years they had moved towards the acceptance of a moral problem and acquired the attitudes and levels of thinking needed to solve it.[9]

A child who is reaching the stage of moral autonomy is establishing a series of principles which become motivating forces for his behaviour when they are incorporated into his picture of himself. Already at the age of nine he has acquired the basic knowledge of his strengths and some grasp of his differences from others upon which, in the following years, he can extend and consolidate his mastery of social situations. He develops more subtle social perception which enables him to respond more effectively to the behaviour of others. He acquires a capacity for greater objectivity which enables him to observe his own actions. His internalized standards provide him with criteria for the assessment of his actions which as they fall short are likely to precipitate guilt feelings and anxiety.

This anxiety is dealt with in two ways. One is the reduction of guilt feelings by confession, apology or restitution which brings the child back to the comfortable position of conformity and moral identification, especially with parents and adults in authority. Confession and restitution may be regarded as a tendency to anticipate the reactions of others' disapproval. They are related to the child's dependency needs and are favoured more by pre-adolescent girls than boys. Such responses are a defensive method of dealing with transgression.

A more powerful, because more internalized, reaction to guilt feelings is self-criticism. The capacity for self-criticism is a product of later social development.[10] It presupposes the emergence of an ideal self. Some of its elements are to be found in the processes of identification with reference figures. Other elements are derived from the learning of the role behaviour of significant others. Whether these roles are instrumental or expressive, their learning depends upon the child's continuing dependency upon his role models. The strength of the dependency leads to the strength of identification, which in turn develops the strength of conscience. Guilt then means the possession of conscious, developmentally advanced, self-critical and self-controlling responses. The self-critical child has developed his self-concept more fully than the child whose responses remain at the level of confession and restitution. Those capable of self-criticism are found to resist temptation more.

The child therefore who has had the normal experiences of home and school during this period is equipped to make autonomous moral judgments and has the self-picture with which to judge his behaviour. Those children in whom the process of socialization has been only partial may show at the worst deviant behaviour, behaviour which violates the norms of the groups to which they belong. It may take the form of socially unacceptable aggression, lack of independence, or outbursts of such symptomatic behaviour as lying or stealing or truancy.

The behaviour may range from transient difficulties in the classroom to delinquency, behaviour which is punishable by law. Most deviant behaviour is derived from a failure to internalize acceptable norms. Sometimes the failure may be the result of an earlier inadequacy of dependency and modelling. The lack of close parental ties, erratic family discipline, and forms of instability in the home are all related to maladaptive behaviour. Delinquency may be due to membership of a subculture in which certain behaviour is accepted that does not conform to the norms of a wider society. It may be due to failure to satisfy the need for achievement in the recognized forms of success in school work or acceptance in normal peer groups. The need for achievement is then transferred to activities which are not acceptable to the school or society at large.[11]

Although most delinquents come to the attention of the authorities when they are adolescent, they generally begin their antisocial activities during middle childhood. The signs that distinguish the more gross forms of deviant behaviour appear as maladaptive behaviour quite early in middle childhood. If the teacher can recognize that cluster of behaviours which includes school misconduct, boredom, failure and the lack of achievement motivation, he may well be able to identify and guide the potentially deviant child before he comes later into the hands of the public authorities.

The child on the other hand whose socialization has proceeded within the range of the norms of accepted behaviour, who has developed confidence and understanding in both his expressive and instrumental roles, and who has built a realistic self-picture of his strengths and weaknesses, is likely to find that he can accept the role demanded by his continuing education in school and find success in it.

Interests, learning and achievement-3

The social experiences of children in later and middle child-hood are woven into a framework of social competence with which they approach new situations. In comparison with the exploratory nature of social relationships in younger children the growth of this framework implies a qualitative change in social interest. It acquires the characteristics of greater per-manence. Group life is more closely identified with the interests which hold members of a group together. Organized groups such as scouts and guides, church organizations and the Junior Red Cross provide a vehicle for this linking of children's groups and their interests. Older children are also aware of the activities of adult society and their interests change as adult interests change. In the Ilford surveys of leisure activities of school children, new interests in non-participant entertainment and in social activities in clubs and coffee bars appeared which were not recorded ten years earlier.[1] Nevertheless the simple categories of interests used in Chapter 8 will provide a preliminary basis on which to examine the changes in older children's interests.

Interests

Physical activities remain a major source of interest and of satisfaction to both boys and girls. They concentrate now upon the acquisition of the finer and more specialized skills. They master the patterns of movement in modern and country dance, the coordination needed to swim well and, in their major interest, football, boys concentrate upon the acquisition of ball-control. They can distinguish between the mastery of a skill and the enjoyment of it which comes from exercising their skills together. The wide individual variation in physical differences among children tends to favour the early maturing child who has a decided advantage in physical strength and skill. This is an important basis of high status in the peer group and of a positive self-picture. The less favoured child may either withdraw from the group, or remain a passive member, or adopt compensatory overactive behaviour within the group.

The form that physical activities take is in part determined by the opportunities in the neighbourhood, such as the presence of water or woodland. In different environments different interests become important. Children in urban areas, who have access to swimming baths, are more likely to develop swimming as a strong interest than those who live in remote hilly areas. These interests are also in part determined by the opportunities offered by their social background. Some engage in horse-riding, others in street games. Parental interest in children can overcome the limitations of the immediate neighbourhood.

The second group of interests falls under the heading of discovery activities which employ skills and knowledge acquired from learning in school and are frequently encouraged by parents at home. The importance of this group of interests, exploring, visiting, collecting and recording is that they provide the first-hand experience, upon which the cognitive development of the children is built. The skills of observation, classification, and recording which are employed in the most extended exploration of these interests are strengthened by a growing capacity for concentration and the increasing satisfaction which comes from the more steady pursuit of the interest. In his earlier years the young child's curiosity embraced the total range of his environment. The interaction between his individual cognitive development, the example of adults, and the common concerns of his peer group leads to a clustering of interests, selective attention to them, and a disciplined curiosity. The measure of an interest is the extent to which it develops the depth and accuracy of knowledge, and the determination to carry it through the problems and periods of difficulty. Children with strong interests learn to acquire the characteristics of task-oriented behaviour.[2]

Discovery activities in a group of children range widely in levels of achievement. One child may be limited to the competitive acquisition of car and train numbers and types. The interest of another child in wild flowers may lead to drawing them and the beginnings of botanical understanding. Such differences depend in part upon the level of cognitive ability which a child can bring to his interest. The choice of interest may be affected by sex typing, in that boys tend to prefer the scientific and mechanical interests of men, and girls those sciences which involve living things.

Sex-differentiated interests are sometime related to the gradual growth of work aspirations in children and limit them. A study of children's work aspirations in a large urban school[3] reported that:

No boys expressed a desire to be nurses, hairdressers, ballet dancers or private secretaries, all of which are included in the girls' list. No girls have indicated any desire to become doctors, or to serve in the Forces or to deliver the post, which are apparently to them masculine occupations.

Their socio-economic background plays an important part in shaping their work aspirations. Children of manual working-class families tend to choose a large number of occupations within a limited social range such as, for boys, postman, bricklayer or taxi driver, and for girls, cinema usherette, kennel maid, hairdresser or typist. Children of middle-class families choose fewer specific occupations, but they are realistic in relation to their family status. In one school population of eleven-year-old girls it was found that ten children from the middle socio-economic ranges could see themselves as teachers for every one child from the lower levels.[4] The way in which the interests of a child are related to work aspirations may be illustrated by the following example:

Margaret, 12 years, the daughter of a cancer research worker, is interested in horses, birds, shells and flowers. She reads nature books and enjoys biology lessons at school. She visits her father's pathology laboratory and would like to be a scientific worker herself in a laboratory like her father's.

The third group of interests is creative and constructive pursuits. These present a complex situation for a child who wishes to be successful in them. On the one hand he has the desire to express that reorganization of experience and feeling which leads to a creative work. On the other hand he brings to bear on the problem it poses him, a number of skills already learnt. Creative work leads to the refinement of perceptual discrimination and experience of the media leads him to the use of a wider range of new skills. Creative and constructional interests of children rank second in strength to their interest in physical activities and outweigh in importance their academic interests, in spite of the fact that they are successful in them.[5] Boys show some decrease in interest in creative work as they grow older, but girls on the other hand, find greater satisfaction in it. Boys tend to turn their energies to model-making and constructional activities including kits, whereas girls tend more than boys to find satisfaction in drawing, painting or writing. When boys declare an interest in woodwork or metalwork and girls in cooking or sewing, the strength of their interest is derived from the creative component of these activities which makes the learning of the appropriate skills possible.

There is also revealed a general tendency in the imaginative life of older children to lose or transform the fantasy elements apparent in the younger age groups. Boys find less satisfaction in the projection of their fantasy life on to model cars and trains, and girls on to dolls and house corner play. The fantasy elements in free writing among the younger children may find expression in writing about dreams and magic. The subject matter popular with the older children often includes death or violence. This is paralleled by the tendency to replace figurative or symbolic painting by representational pictures among the older age group. The thinking that reflected the wishes and fantasies of younger children is modified by the appearance of reality-adjusted thinking as they grow older.

Language and reading

A fourth group of interests centres on language. Language is not only the medium of social communication and learning, it is also the regulator of the child's behaviour. Conversation is adjusted to the environment of people and things. It plays a part in clarifying role-playing, and expressing relationships in situations which match their level of social development. Most children at nine have mastered reading and it becomes an interest for them in its own right. It opens to them a world of people and action beyond their own experience. They may read voraciously, acquiring knowledge which strengthens their other interests.

The continuation of interests which extend children's ability to appreciate and apply the following of rules leads to an increase in the number of games in which they engage, either in pairs or in groups. The popularity of table tennis is due to the opportunity it provides for skilled motor coordination, and competition within a framework of clear rules. Indoor games like Monopoly and card games demand a certain level of intellectual capacity, and some of the most able children begin to discover the challenge of chess.

There is still a wide range of interests to be found in the individual child.

Helen, aged 12 years, listed her interests as:
Music: she played the piano and violin and wanted to join an orchestra; she also read about the lives of composers.
Riding: she possessed a pony, went on pony-trekking holidays, and read stories about horses.
Sketching: landscapes and flowers.
Collecting: bird observations, wild flowers, shells.
Making things: hobby horses from broom handles and stuffed sock heads with wollen manes and stitched eyes. She and her friends used these for mock gymkhanas.
Reading: anything and everything, adventure stories, nature books, history books, books on music and horses.

In this example can also be seen the way in which some of these interests strengthen each other. Helen's wide reading includes material related to her music, riding and collecting. She draws the flowers she has collected and her interest in riding is linked with her constructive work. This clustering of interests is of the greatest importance in providing a basis for children's concern with more specialized knowledge in later childhood.

In the strengthening and deepening interests of children, language plays an important part. It helps to give precision to what they learn and direction to their activities. Language occurs at all levels of complexity. The simplest is where the status differences of those using it are clearly indicated in a primary group, such as father and son in the family, or leader and followers in the peer group. Language which serves to cement these relationships employs only a limited form of expression. The actions and language of its members are related simply to the roles that they play in the primary group. The second purpose of language occurs in wider groups where a different basis of communication has to be established. Events and relationships have to be expressed in sufficient detail to make them intelligible in a wider society. The language used in this case takes on a more objective form detached from the more intimate relationships of the primary group. It enables complex statements about the physical world and the expression of subtleties of feeling to be made.

All children have experience of the first kind of language, at home and with their friends. It is reinforced by the nature of the peer group during these years. Children from more fortunate homes will already have had experience of the second form of language and this is reinforced by the classroom situation in which the class as a whole is larger than any of its friendship subgroups. The pursuit of learning demands the use of language which extends as knowledge increases. Some children, often of lower manual working-class origin, whose families have not introduced them to the forms of language employed by the teacher, find the gap widening between their capacity to profit from education and the work that goes on in the classroom.[6] Their perception of the teacher is limited to the relationship of authority derived from the status of teacher and pupil. Most children, however, are capable of detaching the teacher's activities from his status and can engage in an objective consideration of his actions.

If he will be fair, introduce the class to new and exciting material and be sufficiently emotionally balanced in his dealings with them, the class will then work for him. Such a relationship provides the basis for a bargain between the children and the teacher upon which the discipline of the classroom depends. Children now possess the language with which to express this objectivity. In a class of twelve-year-olds, children commented:

'I like teachers if they are just and fair.'

'I dislike teachers that have favourites and make it obvious in class by asking questions of them more than the others.'

'Teachers should have marvellous knowledge and be able to teach all kinds of children—foreign ones, not very intelligent ones and very brainy ones.'

'He or she must take interesting subjects like science, history, geography, algebra, etc.'

'He cracked excellent jokes about the class nuisances.'

'I didn't like him because when he got angry he used to keep on being angry for the whole of the day.'

Language, as it is used above, not only objectifies the children's relationships with their teacher but clarifies their conception of his role.

Children of eleven and twelve years find in reading a source of interest in its own right. The opportunities they have for wide reading vary considerably. The National Survey undertaken by the Plowden Committee showed that in professional homes 79 per cent of the parents belonged to a library and 95 per cent had more than five books in the home. Only 24 per cent of unskilled parents belonged to a library and 43 per cent had more than five books at home. Of all the homes 29 per cent had five book or less.[7] This differential distribution along socio-economic lines repeats findings ten years earlier.[8] Such differences in opportunities for reading are also related to the kinds of neighbourhood in which children live and often to the streams of the school in which they learn.

Children's knowledge in other fields of interest is extended by the use of books of information. The range of subject matter demanded by a class of children is so wide that it can only be satisfied by adequate provision of a school library and membership of a public library. Boys show an increasing preference for informational books about the physical and mechanical world; they demand illustrations that convey accurate information clearly. On the other hand girls show a greater interest in books about domestic skills, people and their ways of life, and animals. Pets are important to them because they provide objects of social and emotional satisfaction.

Four eleven-year-old girls explained their liking for pets:
'I like dogs when I have no one to play with.'
'He's company and fun to walk with.'
'I like to train him to do tricks.'
'My pets are all very loving and cuddly.'

The differences in reading between boys and girls reflect the differences that have already been shown to exist in their interests.

The tastes of boys and girls in fiction are also marked by differences. Boys prefer stories which offer them clear opportunities for identification in fast-moving action. Although some girls are still reading the myths and fairy stories that satisfied their fantasy needs when they were younger, others are reading stories about human beings, of either their own age or adults, which help their anticipatory socialization into the feminine role.

Comics continue to provide the bulk of the satisfaction of fantasy needs of children of both sexes. This lighter reading changes its nature with increasing age. Boys find their interests served by more specialized journals and an increasing number read about football, hobbies and collecting. Girls derive satisfaction from reading magazines like *Jackie, Petticoat Trend* or *Annabelle*. These serve as an introduction to the world of adolescence, on the threshold of which they stand.

Apart from the service that reading offers to the socialization of children and the enrichment of their interests, it also provides a field for the consolidation of their reading skills. Con-

F

tinuous practice is required to bring a child's reading age to ten years and beyond, the level he has to reach if he is not to slip back into a partial literacy insufficient to cope with the variety of reading situations in a complex society. On the basis of wide practice in the years of middle childhood, he can later acquire the subtler skills of skimming or thorough reading required by different reading situations. The possession of these reading skills is essential to success in secondary and higher education.

Backwardness in reading at this age becomes a major element in the self-picture of the poor reader. His anxiety about failure may already, in the worst cases, have turned into an unfavourable attitude to reading. He may have already decided that his future occupation will be one in which he does not think reading is necessary.[9] His anxieties spread into his relationships with other children. He may become withdrawn. He may be anxious to gain acceptance among them by attracting attention to himself or by adopting a role like that of buffoon which they will accept but which does not contribute towards his own social development. Although each backward reader's performance is the result of a complex of causes, there are certain general common factors to be found in the background of most of them. Poor readers as a group tend to come from larger families of low socio-economic status in which a significant proportion of mothers are out at work all day. Few of the parents belong to public libraries and the books they possess are neither many nor good. Perhaps most important of all the majority of poor readers receive little direct encouragement to read from their parents. In reading as in other forms of learning in school, failure is linked with low levels of parental aspiration, interest and literacy.[10]

Intellectual development

Between the years of nine and thirteen an important change takes place in the mental development of the child. The nine-year-old child organizes his picture of the world through the internalization of logical processes expressed in overt actions. During the next two or three years, each new problem is solved by applying the established framework of concrete operations to it. The variety of strategies which children employ in tackling their problems may be marked by a tendency to be impulsive or reflective in reaching their decisions. This is their individual reaction to the tensions produced by the problem and is a function of their capacity for tolerating ambiguities.[11] The reflective approach grows with increasing age and intellectual maturity, allows new and different intellectual processes to come into play, and generalizes them over a variety of problems.

The most important move forward that the child can take is from the organized understanding of objects and events through concrete operational thought to seeing that the results of the operations can lead to general principles, which might formally be regarded as propositions. Once these higher general propositions are grasped the child can then proceed to relate them together. He discovers that when classification becomes inclusive it is possible to establish an equally inclusive, opposite classification. When a child is faced with a problem, he can now consider more of the different factors involved in solving it so that he can propose several possible solutions. This can only be done when he grasps the variables involved in the problem, realizes the alternative possibilities and prepares a number of hypothetical plans or strategies which he can then test in order to arrive at a satisfactory solution. The mental processes involved in considering the variables in a problem situation begin to show signs of logical thinking in that he comes to manipulate logical relationships such as conjunction, disjunction and implication and to transform them through the operations of negation or reciprocity.[12] The increasing exercise of these processes is accompanied by a detachment from thinking anchored in the concrete world and a subtle shift in emphasis takes place which leads to a growing concern with ideas for their own sake. What makes the cognitive development of children between the years of nine and thirteen interesting is this great move forward towards the building of a framework of complex intellectual processes which will eventually bring their understanding of the world closer to its reality.

Children at thirteen years of age will vary greatly in their development towards the acquisition of these new operations, known as formal operations. Some will still be at the stage of concrete operations. The stage a child has reached is not unrelated to his general level of ability. More important is the mental stimulation and experience offered by his environment, the quality of the language with which he can conceptualize his problems, the expectations made of him, and the social approval which reinforces his success.

The language of individual children at the stage when they are approaching formal operational thought is marked by wide differences which are closely related to their socio-economic levels. By this time the more advanced possess a wide general vocabulary, often enriched by the more specialized vocabularies of their major interests. They are capable of transformation and elaboration on basic sentence types.[13] These children possess the language and can manipulate the symbols which enable them to express the relationships demanded by more advanced processes of thought. Children of lower socio-economic status of the same level of intelligence frequently employ a sentence structure which limits their ability to proceed into more complex relationships of thought.

An example of this may be illustrated from two spoken sentences of similar length by two children of twelve years of comparable measured intelligence:

Maureen, 12 years, L.S.E.S.: 'Everybody looked at me and I walked into the house, and I had a huge bump and I felt sick.'
Rosemary, 12 years, U.S.E.S.: 'Having washed and dressed we proceeded to the dining room which was an elongated room, with gaily coloured curtains and teak tables, Swedish style.'

The four basic syntactic structures used conjunctionally in the first sentence indicate a marked limitation of relationships from which the branching syntactic structure of the second is free. Children of lower socio-economic status tend to employ fewer relative clauses, verbs in the passive mood, adjectival elaborations, adverbial phrases, and other forms of expressing complex relationships. During their years in the junior school, some show in fact an increasing use of conjunctions, repetition of nouns and a reinforcement of ungrammatical constructions.[14]

The close correspondence between the levels of language and the levels of mental development may be illustrated by the variety in the answers given by different children to the following questions:

Where did the earth come from?
Terence, 11 years, 'God made it.'
John, 11 years, 'A large star broke up into nine pieces to form the planets.'

What makes a rainbow?
Sylvia, 12 years, 'The rain and sun together.'
Jonathan, 12 years, 'The sun's white light is composed of seven colours mixed up. A raindrop acts as a prism which the light goes through and it splits up into the different colours.'

Children of similar average measured ability show wide variations in levels of logical thinking.[15] Their ability to think at a certain level in one situation does not mean that they can think at the same logical level in other situations. Educationally subnormal children who come from families of low socio-economic status show no signs of reaching the stage of formal operations. Among these children as old as fifteen years, no higher level of logical thinking is found than that among normal eight-year-old children. On the other hand the highest scores on tests of measured ability do not necessarily predict academic success and eminence in creative public activities.[16]

Achievement motivation

If then there is considerable variation in the achievement of children of average and above average measured ability other factors must be sought to explain these differences. These lie in the development of achievement motivation. The experience of success builds into a consistent pattern of needs and behaviour centred upon the presentation of tasks and problems. The need to achieve is a product of interacting variables.[17] Some of these have been built up through the experiences of the child himself and have become internalized states. Among such are the acceptance of delayed gratification, a level of anxiety which is not too great to interfere with attempting difficult problems or those of a verbal nature, and a preparedness to repeat failures in order to master the problem. Children's own expectations of success or failure, based upon the feed-back of their actual achievement, determine their levels of aspiration. The direction of their aspirations may be affected by sex differences. The need for achievement in boys is directed towards competence for its own sake, whereas the need for achievement in girls is directed towards the adequacy of their social relations.

An illustration of this process may be found in: Barabara, aged 13 years, who had in her junior school written stories which both her teachers and her peers liked. She also wrote similar stories at home which her parents and relatives approved of. At thirteen years she said: 'I shall have to stay on at school, take my 'O' levels, and get one or two 'A' levels, perhaps go on to university and read journalism or take a course at a school of journalism. Then I want to edit my own paper, perhaps in the provinces first then London. My friends have suggested teaching for me as a career, but I don't see myself as a teacher.'

Children's achievement at this age takes place in the setting of their peers. Peer groups often rank athletic prowess higher than academic proficiency and the norms of such groups may lead to the devaluation of academic success. On the other hand peer groups which value success in school may well reward their members' achievement. These peer groups may be differentially influenced by socio-economic factors, or they may compensate for them. By the time children have reached thirteen years of age, the occupation of their fathers is likely to be more significant than their level of measured ability in predicitng children's academic performance.[18] Middle class children are overrepresented in the A streams in schools, more of them stay at school as long as possible, and more of them than would be expected go on to higher education.[19] In a school where special attention is given to high achievers, these environmental factors react with the procedures of the school to increase the motivation of more fortunate children towards success in work at school.

Children before the age of nine years tend to show consistency of attitude across the four chief areas, intellectual, athletic, creative and mechanical, of their activities. A child at this age who is confident of his ability to perform well in one area is likely to expect comparable success in other areas. In the same way a child who is satisfied only by high standards in one area is likely to hold high standards in another. By thirteen years of age, with the experience of a wide range of interests and the growing awareness of his successes and failures in different fields, he develops varying levels of aspiration in these different fields.

Disciplines of learning

The child at school has been brought up against the socially determined usages of reading and the internal consistency of mathematics, against which he must match his own learning. He is already aware of their public context. The older child's exploration of the world becomes more selective as it expands, and he finds that his particular interests lead him to a deepening knowledge of their subject matter. He realizes that this knowledge also is a part of a wider knowledge held by adults or recorded in books beyond the bounds of his firsthand experience. To understand this wider knowledge and relate it to his own, he needs to acquire special methods of thought and special skills appropriate to the subject matter he is interested in. These are of very slow growth and since they inhere in the public forms of knowledge and disciplines of study, they can only be acquired through contact with teachers who themselves have some understanding of the special nature of the fields of knowledge in which the child's interests are set. It therefore becomes appropriate to analyse the further progress of children who have reached this stage under the headings of three chief fields of human knowledge: the understanding of the physical world through science and mathematics; the understanding of the social world through human studies; and the creative activities of the child himself.

During the period of concrete operational thought the child comes to realize the difference between his imaginative and creative activities and his ordering of objective knowledge. The greater the opportunities he has for the discussion of features of his physical environment and experimentation with it in concrete terms of the behaviour of such things as water, air, electricity and metals, the more opportunity he will have of developing the mental operations appropriate to this stage. The methods which adults term scientific begin in very simple situations:

Robert, 11 years, had been predicting which objects float and which sink in water. He had been testing his predictions. He said, 'I have been testing things which float and which do not float. Coke sometimes makes a noise when it is put into the water because water gets into the little holes where the gas is all burnt out. Coke with gas in it sinks, but when the gas is burnt out the coke floats.'

Children's guesses about what will happen are checked by their own experimentation. Their fondness for repeating experiments will lead them on to problems that one experiment alone could not supply. Their records of results help them to compare different situations and to control and direct their thinking. In such ways children grow to understand what accuracy and reliability mean, and they discover what sort of test should be applied to find out whether what they say is true or false. Such an approach ensures that the motivation of their interests is chanelled into appropriate ways of experimenting and discussing physical phenomena. The same principles of questioning, careful observation, discussion and recording apply to the study of natural history.

For some children, among them the less able or environmentally deprived, it may be necessary for the period of gaining fundamental experience to be prolonged. They may reach the stage of formal operations late or perhaps not at all. Other children, abler and older, may show an interest in a wider framework into which their experience fits. This is a state preparatory to the more systematic study based upon some understanding of the nature of scientific enquiry.

The mastery of mathematical concepts, like scientific concepts, is a process of very slow growth. There is a very wide range of achievement in mathematics due to the levels of thinking reached by the child, the attitudes of his parents and peers to the subject, the different expectations made of boys and girls in it, and the understanding of those who teach him.[20] Children of average ability are capable of developing, on an adequate basis of experience, a sound grasp of the common mathematical concepts and relationships.

This takes place when teachers are aware of the underlying structure and pattern of mathematics. They provide the children with structured experiences, the results of which can be recorded in the mathematical symbols which show the relationships being explored. The words proportion, ratio, conservation of area, can have substituted for them the mathematical symbols which generalize these concepts. When children make mistakes they can correct their own thinking; when they are working in groups they can correct each other's thinking. The claims of a fast-developing technological culture demand that as many children as possible should reach this level of competence. In order to reduce the widespread antipathy to mathematics traditionally learned it has become essential that mathematical thinking should replace skill in computation as the objective of children's learning.

The child's understanding of the social world and his interest in other people was satisfied chiefly by stories and descriptions in his early years. In later childhood a more objective content develops. It is at this stage that children find environmental studies satisfying. The place and time in which their world is set becomes an object of study for its own sake. Questions are posed by the artefacts of people in the past and in foreign places and they are answered through firsthand observation and

reference to pictures and books of information. The adult distinction between the study of history and the study of geography must wait upon the development of the appropriate
concepts of time and space in the child.

As children have become acquainted with the historical
figures in the culture of their society their interest extends to
the material conditions under which these figures lived. Provided
with recorded information and acquainted with what objects
survive from the period in which they are interested, they can
become absorbed in the life of a particular period in the past.
Such an interest does not depend upon the existence of a
developed concept of time. It is concerned with the fascination
of the discovery of differences in ways of life between the
present and the past.

Carol, aged 9 years, on her return from school, 'We've been doing
Christopher Columbus and his journey. Do you remember Christopher,
Daddy?'
    Father: 'No, he lived a long time before I was born.'
    Carol: 'Oh, but you remember Jesus, don't you Daddy?'

The concept of time is both complex and of slow growth.
It originates in the repetitive patterns of daily experience and
needs the development of mathematical concepts required for
the measurement of time to provide a framework less egocentric
than personal experience. Although some idea of the past as
opposed to the present is reached at about eight years, the full
understanding of a system of reckoning time is not reached
until about eleven years. The concepts underlying lines of time
and the capacity to represent these, in diagrammatic form, are
not reached until about thirteen years.[21]

The physical life space of the child, the house, the garden,
the classroom, the school and the streets or lanes in which
they are set, is organized into a cognitive map, derived from his
firsthand experiences in moving around this space. The symbolic
representation of the items in a child's cognitive map, the ability
to draw and to understand maps and plans of the area the child
knows well, is likely to be delayed until at least the age of ten

years. Geographical phenomena provide opportunities for comparison, analysis, the establishment of relationships and explanations employing mathematical language, mathematical skills and discussion. Since the concepts of time and space and the symbolic representation of these is later in developing, the children's interests in the material of geographical and historical studies contribute more towards their general intellectual development than to the mastery of the methods of mature historical and geographical disciplines.

Creative achievement

The creative activities of the child himself continue to be a major source of interest through later childhood. For most children the maintenance of this interest depends not upon the opportunities offered by their homes but upon the provision of space and materials in the school and upon the teacher's understanding of what the children can do with these facilities. Working space and equipment for art and movement, the quiet demanded by creative writing, and the instruments essential to music making are the responsibility of the school. Creative activities for older children therefore take place within the culture of the school itself, and they flourish according to the value placed upon them by the school.

Children show maturational changes through an increasing differentiation and subtlety in the perceptual modalities employed in different forms of creative work. Children in their work in painting and modelling move from a schematic ordering of symbols to a desire to pattern details which bear some resemblance to the real appearance of objects. The exaggeration in size which at an earlier stage indicated the relative importance of the objects is frequently replaced by concentration on detail for the same purpose.[22] They are also able to respond to the internal qualities of natural forms, machinery and buildings and derive satisfaction in constructing non-representational products or painting abstract pictures. In their observations of these objects they discover systems of relationships upon which they operate so that they create new products. While at one time a child is engaged in exploring relationships of form and colour, he will at another time be interpreting the world with intense realism. A desirable artistic environment in school presents children with opportunities to experiment in modelling, carving, constructing, graphic work and work with textiles. Each of these media offers a variety of artistic problems in a context of feeling and in their solution children acquire the skills necessary for communicating their interpretation of the world.

A second field of creative work in which the interaction of the children's development and interest with the opportunities offered by the school is important is their original writing. Under favourable conditions, they continue to enjoy the expression of their characteristic zest for living.

Bernard, aged 10 years, wrote

Things I Like

I like the sound of a steam engine as it roars through a tunnel,
The shriek of its whistle as it stops in a station.
I like to watch the seagulls flying
As they soar and glide and sway.
I like the noise the sea makes as it hits the shore,
The ripple on the stones and sand.
I like horses as they gallop along.
I like the feel of the wind so strong.
I like the streamline look of a plane
as it flies through the air.
I like the shape of a hull of a ship.
A ship that floats in the sea.
I like the feel of a very soft bed
And a soft pillow on which I rest my head.
All these are things I like.

Important elements in encouraging creative writing are the permissiveness of the classroom situation, which tends to develop word fluency, and the sensitivity of the teacher to words and images. A teacher who encourages his children to translate their images into words, provides constant feedback and appreciation, and enriches the children's imagination by reading to them, provides a positive influence in the constant interaction between children, stimulus and teacher. The effect of the variables, verbal ability, positive teacher influence, and a permissive situation is likely to produce work of high creative quality. Two examples of creative writing, one of prose, one of verse, which have arisen from such a situation follow:

Malcolm, aged 11 years, wrote 'Sacrifice to the Gods' after hearing 'Chano' by Johnny Dankworth.

'I was in the middle of dense, African jungle, and was looking down, under the light of a brilliant moon, on to a rough camp, a large fire brilliantly burning in the centre. It was surrounded by reed huts, and a mumbling of voices came from within. Suddenly an elegant, tall, male figure came strolling out, followed by a host of other natives, wildly dressed. The tall man had a large brilliantly coloured mask over his face. More Negroes came out, with an everlasting variety of musical instruments, ranging from a twisted horn, to two branches. With a deep rumble, the drums began and a squealing baby elephant was driven towards the fire. The horns blew, and the elephant squealed madly for its mother. The strangely dressed natives hopped from one foot to another, leaping wildly into the air, closing in on the frightened beast. They bent sideways, so that both hands touched the ground. They then proceeded to do cartwheels constantly keeping in a perfect circle whilst the tall man threw his arms up to the fire. The dancing stopped suddenly and a peculiar deathly silence filled the jungle. The poor beast was driven into the flames and burnt alive. The fire crackled away at the corpse. The natives returned to their huts, and hours later the fire died down, to leave only charred remains of the night's passing. The sun rose, dawn cracked, and another day began. A shaft of sunlight fell on my face, causing me to awake with a start. I glanced at my bedside clock. 'Gracious!' I exclaimed: 'I've overslept!'

Graham, aged 11 years, wrote:

The Train
Perhaps a plunge of a carp
after the flies which are
hovering over the water, is heard.
A valley is formed.
The peaks are endless
stretching their night gowns and hats
to the sky.

Willows shade the frisky ponies.
A tuft of cotton is blown past
a fox's hole.
The young ones pounce
and leap after it.
The silence is broken by a trail
of legs and eyes.
His breath blackened
The steel monster thundered.
It's gone once more
The peace is here.

The learning of children between the ages of nine and thirteen years does not move forward on a straight front. In some areas of cognitive learning, certain levels of conceptual development are more advanced than in others. The successful child of thirteen can employ a framework of mathematical concepts which has developed over a long period of time. His scientific concepts are likely to be less complete and more difficult to use. Concepts of time and space are of recent growth. Although there is a tendency for him to perceive the world with greater objectivity, the levels he has reached at thirteen years will vary from one field of activity to another. In mathematics and science he has already realized that the criteria for judging truth or falsity inhere in the public cultural heritage of which he is a part. In some of his learning he has already made contact with the forms of knowledge, appreciated the nature of the evidence with which they work, and the characteristic methods of their pursuit.[23] In others he is not yet ready to comprehend the forms of knowledge into which his learning might be divided.

The mastery of the organization of conceptual cognitive knowledge may seem to imply that the learner must adopt an attitude of conformity to the learning situation. This conformity would seem to be a necessary element in the good pupil role and in so far as this role implies achievement according to the accepted standards of the school, a high degree of social adjustment and the internalization of the norms of adults, the good pupil role makes little allowance for able children whose mental functioning is less predictable. Such children possess to a marked degree the qualities of mind of the divergent thinker whose fluency and flexibility of ideas enable him to produce unexpected relationships and novel solutions.[24] Their needs are not met in the same way as those of the conventional good pupil are met.

In a suggestive study by Wallach and Kogan of eleven-year-old children an attempt was made to group children according to their scores on tests of measured ability and tests of creative thinking.[25] Gifted children with high scores on both tests need a teacher whose flexibility of mind and acceptance of the unconventional will match their own. When the children become aware of their own gifts at about eleven years, they begin to find satisfaction in the company of children of comparable talents. Within these peer groups they use a high level of language in order to share and assess with each other their experiments in divergent thinking. If a gifted child is with peers who cannot follow the quickness and variety of his thought he may realize his difference from them and become separate or even isolated. He is not likely to be chosen as highly popular by the rest of the class. If the gifted child learns under conditions favourable for his development, he has much to offer that may well be overlooked if the school's conception of achievement is limited to the more conventional criteria of success in its work.

Children who score highly on tests of measured ability but less on tests of creativity are successful in conventional school work and show little anxiety. They are regarded favourably by their teachers because they get things right in the way the teacher has prescribed. Greater difficulties occur for children of high creativity and low intelligence. Their cognitive disfunctioning leads them to feelings of failure in conventional school work and in competition for achievement. They may find satisfaction in expressive activities divorced from measured academic success like art or movement. On the other hand those who are low both in intellectual power and creativity show the highest levels of anxiety. They may find compensation in social activity like dancing and singing or in rowdyism. They may become apathetic or aggressive.

The achievement of children does not bear a simple relationship with any single measure of ability. It is the product of psychological and social forces which influence the whole range of behaviour of the child. The identification of the relationships between these forces provides further lines of guidance for those procedures which will satisfy the variety of children's needs.

Some implications for the education of the child in the middle school

The social development of children in the pre-adolescent years can be regarded as a stage distinct from the exploratory stage which precedes it and the adolescent stage which is directed towards the establishment of a permanent identity and the roles appropriate to work and marriage. The middle period is devoted to the definition of sex roles and role play within single sex groups. Older children are extending their interests and gaining a sense of achievement through them. They are setting levels of aspiration for themselves and developing a realistic self-picture. Their reference groups are extended beyond the family to their peer groups and they find new individuals as models with which to identify. The social competence they achieve is a crucial variable affecting their achievement in school.

A second variable is to be found in the levels of intellectual development they reach. Some remain throughout this period at the level of concrete operational thought. Others are in a transitional stage to formal operational. thought for they are capable of this later stage in some fields of intellectual activity but remain at the earlier stage in others. The importance of this period of transition suggests that children should be helped through it by methods of teaching in an environment planned to that end.

The social and intellectual development of children which is regarded as the particular function of the school does not take place in isolation from the society of which the school is a major institution. Rapid technological change is tending to make less appropriate the early selection of children to learn the special skills demanded by the work of society a generation ago. In industrial societies the period during which comprehensive education takes place tends to become longer. This enables decisions about future education and training to be more realistic. It provides a longer time for general education in which children may learn how to think, before they are committed to the highly specialized skills demanded by a society based on the extreme division of labour. This movement is exemplified by those comprehensive secondary schools with a common curriculum up to the age of thirteen years before vocational and educational choices are made.

The Scottish Council for Research in Education has concluded that there is no 'correct' age for the transfer of children from primary education associated with concrete operational thinking to secondary education associated with specialization and formal operational thinking. The ages from ten to thirteen years should be regarded as a period of transition which implies a gradual change in curriculum and style of teaching.[1] If this change is accepted, a school can be devised which would satisfy the needs of children up to the age of thirteen years. The recommendation of the Plowden Committee that the age of transfer to secondary education should be twelve years rather than thirteen is based chiefly on administrative grounds, though its recommendation in favour of a middle school for English children is in line with the general trends to be found in most complex societies.

The major problem posed by the organization of the middle school is that of ensuring that children move forward from the best practices of primary schools to the satisfaction of their needs for a deeper understanding in the various areas of knowledge. At nine years of age their learning does not differentiate subject from subject. At thirteen years of age some children still need a form of teaching which continues the approach of the good primary school. Others have reached a level of thinking in some areas of knowledge which can only be satisfied by an introduction to the discipline of the subject. The satisfaction of these needs can be achieved by teachers who are rooted in the best primary approaches and are capable of contributing specialist enthusiasm and knowledge to the older pupils, and by an organization which extends beyond the traditional allocation of one teacher to each class. It requires also the material facilities and replanning of buildings to allow for the pursuit of children's interests in groups of varying size.

In these circumstances the diffuse role of the teacher, appropriate to the first school, undergoes a change. Because of the importance of the social cohesion in which the development of these children takes place, the identity of the class and its relationship with one teacher must provide the basis of the formal structure of the middle school. The instructional role of the teacher no longer implies that he should be able to teach everything to all the children in his class. He can only satisfy their deepening interests if he makes himself an authority in one or two cognate subjects. A teacher interested in English, history and geography, or in science, mathematics or rural studies would be more equipped to carry the interests of the older children further in certain directions, than a general class teacher. This implies that the staff of the middle school should consist of a balanced team of teachers whose enthusiasms cover the range of children's interests. They will not teach as specialists. The compartmentalized knowledge embodied in a syllabus based upon the internal logic of a subject is inappropriate to the needs of the children who are not ready for the fragmented timetable of the traditional secondary school curriculum. Nevertheless a degree of flexibility in the use that teachers make of their time and in the timetable is required, so that they may help in refining the children's operations of thought and lead them towards the ordering of their knowledge. For the older children this is an essential step towards the growth of that understanding in which new knowledge takes its place. The Department of Education and Science, in its proposals for middle schools, considers that the school is likely to be more generously staffed, with classes of about thirty-five children.[2] This will allow for teaching groups to vary in size in order to cope with the increasing range of attainment found within one age group. A more generous allowance of staff would then permit such experiments as team teaching, recommended in the Plowden Report, to take place.

A mixed staff would allow for identification figures of both sexes to be available to children, and in a mixed school the opportunities for boys and girls to learn side by side may soften the grosser forms of sex role identification found in single sex schools.

The middle school would be a place where children would have an unbroken opportunity to develop their social life and pursue their learning through deepening interests helped by teachers with firmly grounded and disciplined knowledge. The buildings of the primary school do not normally provide space or equipment for groups of children to pursue a continuing study in which they have found absorbing interest. On the other hand the specialized rooms of the secondary school make no provision for the relatedness of these children's activities. The proposals of the Department of Education and Science for building middle schools suggest ways of extending existing junior schools to increase and differentiate the use of space in them. Each of these suggestions provides for the close relationship between a group of subjects; in one example mathematics, science, study space and workshop crafts are combined in a block of new buildings under a team of three teachers. In another block, provision is made for English, drama, a second language with a language laboratory and art and craft, in the charge of another team of three teachers. Extensions to existing buildings suffer from the limitation that once the rooms are equipped for their various purposes, they crystallize relationships between the subjects and ways of teaching them. This can be avoided where middle schools are planned as new schools. Here the Department's proposals assume that the school will be divided into year groups of pupils ranging in size from 70 to 140 pupils with a member of staff for each 35 pupils. The year groups share such common facilities as hall, dining room, library, space for movement, playing fields and, if the school is fortunate, a swimming bath. Each year group will have in addition its own centre. The group of younger children will spend more time in classes of thirty-five in their centre than the older children, but the informal arrangement of their classrooms and the provision of study bays and areas for practical work will enable the classes to engage in group work. It is expected that the older children will more rarely spend time in groups of thirty-five and the buildings of their centre therefore will only provide four rooms each seating that number of pupils. Since there are spaces equipped for study, with books for social studies, for mathematics and science, and for art and both light and heavy crafts, with facilities for ready access from one to the other, there is adequate space for a large number of children to be pursuing a variety of interests under at least four teachers who contribute from their expertise to a team responsible for planning the curriculum.

At this age the children's learning is powerfully affected by this flexibility of arrangement. It enables grouping on the basis of interest rather than ability to take place. Reference has already been made to the self-fulfilling prophecy implicit in ability grouping and streaming which leads children in the upper streams of ability to improve their performance and those in the lower streams to deteriorate. The children will be working in groups according to their interests and not according to the way they have been allotted to A or C streams. The abler children will progress in the context of their group's activities, not in the context of the class. The less able children, who will be found mostly among the slow readers, will show their relative backwardness by nine years of age. The present organization of schools means that children identified as backward are often moved to the secondary school before they have had enough time to establish their reading skills securely. A quarter of the pupils in secondary modern schools fail to achieve an acceptable level of literacy at fifteen years of age.[3] The middle school provides the opportunity, if necessary, of up to four years' remedial work under a specialist.

The role of the teacher in the middle school will show significant changes from that of the teacher in the first school. His role set will be different. He will be working with other members of staff who can claim, like himself, expertise in academic subjects, practical activities, or special methods of teaching, such as those needed in the language laboratory or in the backward group. The parents of the children will tend to make more specific demands upon the school according to the aspirations of their subculture. They will vary in the expectations they hold about the child's progress. One of the functions of the teacher is to explain to parents what is taking place in the school, for many parents base their expectations for their children upon their own experience of school a generation before. The stages of social and mental development of children in the middle school make different demands upon the teacher from those in the first school. Their relationship with him is successful in so far as he offers them stability, recognizes their strong group affiliations, and meets their growing intellectual needs. Within the more flexible arrangement of buildings and furniture in the school, his roles are more complex and varied. Each different arrangement of chairs and table suggests different forms of communication within the group of which he is a member. As the room arrangement changes from a series of tables each with a small group of four children working together, to chairs in a semicircle to provide an audience for children's dramatic work, so the role of the teacher changes. In one arrangement he may be called in to help, but the initiative rests with the children. In another he may well be turned to by the rest of the group as an expert. In another he may be another member of the audience. These roles are an extension of his instructional role, ensuing a framework within which learning can take place.

Children in the middle school would be more consciously coming to grips with the world as it is. The instructional role of the teacher would be more than the transmission of the skills and knowledge of the culture, because the culture itself is rapidly changing. The gap between the teacher and his children is the result of rapid change rather than the normal difference between the generations. Not only is the material environment different, but the opportunities for social mobility steadily increase with the growth of the salaried middle class. The school reaches into wider sections of the community, participates actively in social change and prepares its pupils for rising standards and increasing cultural opportunity. The teacher's skill depends on his understanding of these pressures on the children. The professional role implies more the application of the findings of research to the changing background of children, to the children themselves and to the ways in which they learn. Teachers of children in the middle school would need also to keep the knowledge they offer to the children up-to-date as technical advances invade the material and methods of their special field. This is already seen in the work of such bodies as the Schools Council and the Nuffield Foundation, concerned with the reconsideration of curricula. The importance of their proposals lies in a recognition of the need to reshape the preparation of children for a world in which understanding and flexibility of mind are more appropriate than the skills and knowledge of an earlier generation. The middle school will be deeply affected by these curricular changes and it will make new demands upon its teachers in that the teacher has to maintain his professional role and allow it to change as schools and society change.

Proposals for the reorganization of education which would lead to a first school and a middle school are an example of the changes in education which stem from the shifting emphases in society as a whole. The demand is now for a longer period of preparation and the fuller use of the talents of the members of contemporary society. The middle school would delay the age of selection and continue the comprehensive nature of the present primary school to thirteen years. The pre-adolescent period from the beginning of school life to the age of thirteen, may be regarded as a period of growth within which a developmental break takes place around the age of nine years. Increasing knowledge of the nature of children's social development and its relationship to achievement suggests such important differences between a child of seven and a child of eleven that separate schools should cater for these separate stages. Proposals for first and middle schools, in the West Riding[4] and elsewhere, are based on these assumptions, and their implementation will be effective in so far as those responsible for them have rethought how to meet the needs of the children in the schools.

References

PART I The pre-school child

Chapter I The socialization of the pre-school child

1 S. Cotgrove, *The Science of Society*, Allen & Unwin, 1967, chapter 2.
2 J. Bowlby, *Maternal Care and Mental Health*, W.H.O. 1951, Part 1; see also M. D. Ainsworth. 'The effects of maternal deprivation', in *Deprivation of Maternal Care and Reassessment of its Effects*, W.H.O., 1962.
3 J. H. Clausen and J. Williams. 'Sociological correlates of child behaviour', in H. W. Stevenson, ed., *Child Psychology*, 62nd Year Book of the Nat. Soc. for the Study of Education: Part I, Chicago University Press, 1963, pp. 93-4.
4 J. H. Clausen and J. Williams. 'Sociological correlates of child behaviour', in H. W. Stevenson, ed., *Child Psychology*, 1963, p. 91.
5 J. G. Howells, *Family Psychiatry*, Oliver & Boyd, 1963.
6 D. E. May, *Children in the Nursery School*, University of London Press, 1963, pp. 41-8.
7 M. Young and P. Willmott, *Family and Kinship in East London*, Routledge, 1957, chapter 3.

Chapter 2 Socialization and the development of personality

1 K. M. B. Bridges, 'Emotional development', in *Child Development*, vol. 3, 1932, pp. 324-41.
2 W. W. Hartup, 'Dependence and independence', in H. W. Stevenson, ed., *Child Psychology*, 1963, pp. 356-7.
3 A. Bandura and R. H. Walters, *Social Learning and Personality Development*, Holt, Rinehart & Winston, 1964, pp. 146-48.
4 A. T. Jersild. 'Emotional development', in L. Carmichael, ed., *Manual of Child's Psychology*, Wiley, 1946, pp. 769-73.
5 H. W. Stevenson, 'Development psychology', in *Annual Review of Psychology*, 1967, p. 105.

6 J. & E. Newsom, *Infant Care in an Urban Community*. Allen & Unwin, 1963, chapter 11.

7 A. Bandura and R. H. Walters, 'Aggression', in H. W. Stevenson, ed., *Child Psychology*, 1963, p. 358.

8 B. K. Ruebush, 'Anxiety', in H. W. Stevenson, ed., *Child Psychology*, 1963, pp. 460-504.

Chapter 3   The development of attitudes

1 M. Jahoda and N. Warren, *Attitudes*, Penguin, 1966, Part I.

2 D. E. May, *Children in the Nursery School*, University of London Press, 1963, p. 23.

3 P. Y. Galpfrin, 'An experimental study in the formation of mental actions,' in B. Simon, ed., *Psychology in the Soviet Union*, Routledge, 1957, pp. 219-22.

4 M. E. Eson, *Psychological Foundations of Education*, Holt, Rinehart & Winston, 1965, pp. 399-413.

5 V. J. Crandall, 'Achievement', in H. W. Stevenson, ed., *Child Psychology*, 1963, pp. 424-32.

6 B. Bernstein, 'Social structure, language and learning', in M. Craft, et al., *Linking Home and School*. Longmans, 1962.

7 Central Advisory Council for Education, *Children and Their Primary Schools*, H.M.S.O. 1967, vol. 2, Table 19, p. 117.

8 D. McCarthy, 'Language development in children', in L. Carmichael, ed., *Manual of Child Psychology*. Wiley, 1946, p. 530.

9 F. E. Merrill, *Society and Culture*, 3rd. ed., Prentice-Hall, 1965, pp. 158-63.

10 For a recent discussion of this problem see: R. F. Dearden, 'The concept of play', in R. S. Peters, ed., *The Concept of Education*, 1967, Routledge.

11 E. J. Gibson, 'Perceptual development', in H. W. Stevenson, ed., *Child Psychology*, 1963, pp. 189-90.

12 E. J. Gibson, 'Perceptual development', in H. W. Stevenson, ed., *Child Psychology*, 1963, pp. 160-6.

13 As, for example, in: A. Gesell, 'The autogenesis of infant behaviour', in L. Carmichael, ed., *Manual of Child Psychology*, Wiley, 1946, pp. 299-307.

14 M. M. Lewis, *Language, Thought and Personality in Infancy and Childhood*, Harrap, 1963, chapter 4.

Chapter 4   Interests, learning and achievement - I

1 For a philosophical treatment of the concept of interest see : R. S. Peters, *Ethics and Education*, Allen & Unwin, 1966, chapter 6.
2 K. Chukovsky, *From Two to Five*, California University Press, 1963, chapter 4.
3 E. Stones, *An Introduction to Educational Psychology*, Methuen (University Paperbacks), 1966, pp. 81-5.
4 J. Piaget, *The Origins of Intelligence in the Child*, Int. University Press, 1952, pp. 147-8.
5 J. H. Flavell, *The Developmental Psychology of Jean Piaget*, Van Nostrand, 1963, p. 155.
6 A. A. Liublinskaya, 'The development of children's speech and thought', in B. Simon, ed., *Psychology in the Soviet Union*, Routledge, 1957.
7 J. G. Wallace, *Concept Growth and the Education of the Child*, National Foundation for Educational Research, Newnes, 1965, pp. 148-50.
8 V. J. Crandall, 'Achievement', in H. W. Stevenson, ed., *Child Psychology*, 1963, pp. 416-19.
9 M. L. Kellmer Pringle, *Deprivation and Education*, Longmans, 1965, chapter 2.

Chapter 5   Some implications for the education of the pre-school child

1 Central Advisory Council for Education, *Children and Their Primary Schools*. H.M.S.O., 1967, vol. 1, p. 124.
2 W. D. Wall, *The Enrichment of Childhood*. Nursery Schools' Association, 1960.
3 W. Van der Eyken, *The Pre-school Years*, Penguin, 1967, p. 94.
4 Central Advisory Council for Education, *Children and Their Primary Schools*, H.M.S.O., 1967, vol. 1, chapter 9.

PART II   The child from five to nine
Chapter 6   Children entering school

1 M. C. Templin, *Certain Language Skills in Children*, University of Minnesota Press, 1957, chapter 5.
2 W. A. L. Blyth, *English Primary Education*, Routledge, 1965, vol. 1, pp. 165, 169.

3 Central Advisory Council for Education, *Children and Their Primary Schools*. H.M.S.O., 1967, vol. 1, p. 138.
4 P. H. Mussen, J. J. Conger and J. Kagan, *Child Development and Personality*, Harper and Row, 1963, pp. 326-30.

Chapter 7 Roles and attitudes - I

1 For a treatment of the importance of social perception see: D. Kretch, R. S. Crutchfield and E. L. Ballachey, *Individual and Society*, McGraw-Hill, 1962, pp. 51-65.
2 W. A. L. Blyth, *op. cit.*, vol. 1. pp. 47-8, vol. 2, pp. 49-60.
3 R. C. Johnson and G. R. Medinnus, *Child Psychology*, Wiley, pp. 277-97.
4 B. Bernstein, 'Social class and linguistic development', A. H. Halsey, J. Floud and C. A. Anderson, eds., in *Education, Economy and Society*, Glencoe Free Press, 1963, pp. 292-6.
5 J. Klein, 'The parents of school children', in M. Craft, *et al.*, *Linking Home and School*, Longmans, 1967.
6 Central Advisory Council for Education, *op. cit.*, 1967, vol. 2, pp. 184-9.
7 V. Crandall, S. Orieans, A. Preston and A. Rabston, 'The development of social compliance in children', in *Child Development*, vol. 29, 1958.
8 P. H. Mussen, *et. al.*, *op. cit.*, pp. 379-92.
9 M. E. Eson, *Psychological Foundations of Education*, Holt, Rinehart & Winston, 1965, pp. 74-8.
10 W. A. L. Blyth, *op. cit.*, vol. 1, 1965, pp. 74-8.
11 Talcott Parsons, 'The school class as a social system', in A. H. Halsey J. Floud and C. A. Anderson, eds., *Education, Economy and Society*, 1963, p. 440.
12 L. Kohlberg, 'Moral development and indentification', in H. W. Stevenson, ed., *Child Psychology*, 1963, pp. 424-32. See also L. Bloom, 'Piaget's theory of the development of moral judgment', in M. Jahoda, and N. Warren, *Attitudes*, Penguin, 1966, pp. 116-24.
13 M. L. Kellmer Pringle, *Deprivation and Education*. Longmans, 1965, chapter 3.
14 B. K. Ruebush, 'Anxiety', in H. W. Stevenson, ed., *Child Psychology*, Chicago University Press, 1963, pp. 489-501.
15 M. L. Kellmer Pringle, *op. cit.*, pp. 28 and 49.

Chapter 8   Interests, learning and achievement - 2

1 Compare the treatment of children's interests in E. W. Hughes, 'Children's choices in individual activities in the junior school', *Brit. J. of Educ. Psych.*, vol. 25, 1955.

2 R. Dottrens, *The Primary School Curriculum*, UNESCO, 1962, pp. 168-73.

3 See B. Inhelder and J. Piaget, *The Growth of Logical Thinking from Childhood to Adolescence*, Basic Books, 1958.

4 A. R. Luria, 'The role of speech in the formation of temporary connections', in B. Simon, ed., *Psychology in the Soviet Union*, Routledge, 1955, p. 119.

5 M. C. Templin, *Certain Language Skills in Children*, University of Minneapolis Press, 1957, pp. 149-57.

6 W. Jeffrey, 'Variables in early discrimination learning', *Child Development*, vol. 29, 1958.

7 For a brief summary of current practice and problems in reading see: Central Advisory Council for Education, *Children and Their Primary Schools*, H.M.S.O., 1967, vol. 1, pp. 211-16.

8 J. M. Morris, *Reading in the Primary School*, Newnes, 1959, vol. 1, p. 104.

9 Central Advisory Council for Education, *Children and Their Primary Schools*, H.M.S.O., 1967, vol. 1, p. 213.

10 D. Schonfield, 'Special difficulties at a reading age of 8+', *Brit. J. of Educ. Psych.*, vol. 26, 1956, Part I.

11 For a discussion of this problem see: R. J. Goldman, *Religious Thinking from Childhood to Adolescence*. Routledge, 1964.

12 K. Melzi, *Art in the Primary School*, Blackwell, 1967, pp. 6-7.

13 E. P. Torrance, *Guiding Creative Talent*, Prentice-Hall, 1964, chapter 3.

14 J. S. Bruner, 'The act of discovery', in R. C. Anderson and D. P. Ausubel, *Readings in the Psychology of Cognition*, Holt, Rinehart & Winston, 1961.

15 See for example: Nuffield Mathematics Project, *I Do, and I Understand*, Chambers and Murray, 1967.

16 K. Lovell, *The Growth of Basic Mathematical and Scientific Concepts in Children*, University of London Press, 1961. chapter 4.

Chapter 9 Some implications for the education of the child between five and nine years

1 Talcott Parsons, 'The school class as a social system', in A. H. Halsey, J. Floud and C. A. Anderson, eds., *Education, Economy and Society*, 1963, p. 445.

2 M. A. Mycock, 'A comparison of vertical grouping and horizontal grouping in the infant school', in *Brit. J. Educ. Psych.*, 37, 1967, p. 1.

3 V. Southgate, 'Approaching i.t.a. results with caution', *Educational Research*, vol. 7, (2), 1965.

4 E. M. Williams and H. B. Shuard, *Primary Mathematics Today*, Longmans.

5 Central Advisory Council for Education, *Children and Their Primary Schools*, H.M.S.O., 1967, vol. 1, pp. 287-93.

6 *Ibid.*, p. 136.

7 C. J. Willig, 'Social implications of streaming in the junior school', in *Educational Research*, vol. 5 (2), 1963.

8 Central Advisory Council for Education, *Primary Education in Wales*, H.M.S.O., 1967, chapter 20.

9 B. Wilson, 'The teacher's role: a sociological analysis', *Brit. J. of Sociology*, vol. 13, 1962.

PART III The child from nine to thirteen

Chapter 10 Socialization in the pre-adolescent years

1 T. Parsons, 'The school class as a social system', in A. H. Halsey, J. E. Floud and C. A. Anderson, eds., *Education, Economy and Society*, 1961.

2 R. C. Johnson and G. R. Medinnus, *Child Psychology: Behaviour and Development*, 1965, chapter 2, Wiley.

3 I. Opie and P. Opie, *The Lore and Language of School Children*, O.U.P., 1958.

4 G. H. Mead, *Mind, Self and Society*, Chicago University Press, 1934, p. 162.

5 L. Kohlberg, 'Moral development and identification', in H. W. Stevenson, ed., *Child Psychology*, 1963, p. 316.

6 T. Parsons, *The Social System*, Routledge, 1964, pp. 48-9.

7 F. Musgrove, 'The social needs and satisfactions of some young people', *Brit. J. Educ. Psych.*, 36 (1).

8 W. A. L. Blyth, *English Primary Education: A Sociological Description*, Routledge, 1965, vol. 1, chapter 3.

9 P. H. Mussen, J. J. Conger and J. Kagan, *Child Development and Personality*, 2nd. edn., Harper & Row, 1963, chapters 11, 15.

10 A. N. Smith, 'A survey of the attainments and interests of ten year old children from differing geographical environments within a county', In *Brit. J. Educ. Psych.*, 33 (3), 1963.

Chapter 11   Roles and attitudes - 2

1 S. Gooch and M. L. Kellmer Pringle, *Four Years On*, National Bureau for Co-operation in Child Care, Research Report No. 1, Longmans, 1965, pp. 64-75.

2 J. Kagan and B. Henker, 'Developmental psychology', in *Annual Review of Psychology*, vol. 17, 1966, pp. 34-5.

3 L. Stenhouse, *Culture and Education*, Nelson, 1967, chapter 7.

4 J. W. B. Douglas, *The Home and the School*, MacGibbon & Kee, pp. 114-15.

5 S. Cotgrove, *The Science of Society: An Introduction to Sociology*, Allen & Unwin, 1967, p. 90.

6 L. Kohlberg, 'Moral development and indentification', in H. W. Stevenson, ed., *Child Psychology*, 1963, p. 323.

7 B. Bernstein, 'Social class and linguistic development: a theory of social learning', in A. H. Halsey, J. Floud and C. A. Anderson, eds., *Education, Economy and Society*, 1963, pp. 292-4.

8 E. K. Wilson, *Sociology: Rules, Roles and Relationships*. Dorsey Press, 1966, chapter 3.

9 R. T. Seville, 'Some categories of thinking, revealed in problem-solving by children in the junior school', unpublished diploma dissertation, Cambridge Institute of Education, 1964.

10 L. Kohlberg, 'Moral development and identification' in H. W. Stevenson, ed., *Child Psychology*, 1963, pp. 291-2.

11 S. Cotgrove, *The Science of Society: An Introduction to Sociology*, Allen & Unwin, 1967, pp. 290-5.

Chapter 12   Interests, learning and achievement - 3

1 M. Stewart, *The Leisure Activities of School Children*. Workers' Educational Association, 1948 and 1958.

2 R. S. Peters, *Ethics and Education*. Allen & Unwin, 1966, pp. 78-9.

3 E. M. Harper, 'The leisure activities of two age-groups of primary school children', unpublished diploma dissertation, Cambridge Institute of Education, 1966.

4 *Ibid.*

5 K. M. Evans, *Attitudes and Interests in Education*, Routledge, 1965, p. 113.

6 B. Bernstein, 'Social class and linguistic development: a theory of social learning', in A. H. Halsey, J. Floud and C. A. Anderson, eds., *Education, Economy and Society*, pp. 304-7.

7 Central Advisory Council for Education, *Children and Their Primary Schools*, H.M.S.O., 1967, vol. 2, p. 116.

8 J. D. Carsley, 'The interests of children (ages 10-11) in books', *Brit. J. Educ. Psych.* vol. 27 (1), 1957.

9 J. M. Morris, *Standards and Progress in Reading*, Nat. Foun. for Educ. Research, 1966, p. 186.

10 Central Advisory Council for Education, *Children and Their Primary Schools*, vol. 1, pp. 36-6.

11 J. Agan and B. Henke, 'Developmental psychology', in *Annual Review of Psychology*, vol. 17, 1966, p. 26.

12 J. H. Flavell, *The Developmental Psychology of Jean Piaget*, Van Nostrand, 1963, pp. 212-22.

13 J. B. Carrol, *Language and Thought*, Prentice-Hall, 1964, chapter 2.

14 G. F. Fisher, 'A study of linguistic development in the junior school', unpublished diploma dissertation. Cambridge Institute of Education, 1967.

15 S. Jackson, 'The growth of logical thinking in normal and subnormal children', *Brit. J. Educ. Psych.*, vol. 35 (2), 1965.

16 F. V. Smith, 'Critical notice'. *Brit. J. Educ. Psych.*, vol. 36 (3) 1966.

17 V. J. Crandall, 'Achievement', in H. W. Stevenson, ed., *Child Psychology*, 1963, pp. 432-5.

18 *Ibid.*, p. 425.

19 Douglas, *op. cit.*

20 D. M. Lee, *Background to Mathematical Development*. Oldbourne, 1962, p. 218.

21 J. G. Wallace, *Concept Growth and the Education of the Child*, Nat. Found. Ed. Research, 1965, pp. 122-30.

22 K. Melzi, *Art in the Primary School*, Blackwell, 1967, pp. 17-20.

23 P. H. Hirst, 'The logical and psychological aspects of teaching a subject', in R. S. Peters, ed., *The Concept of Education*, Routledge, 1967.

24 J. P. Guilford, 'Parameters and categories of talent', in *Year Book of Education*, Evans, 1962.

25 M. A. Wallach and N. Kogan, *Modes of Thinking in Young Children*, Wiley, 1965.

Chapter 13 Some implications for the education of the child in the middle school

1 J. D. Nisbet and N. J. Entwistle, *The Age of Transfer to Secondary Education*, University of London Press, 1966, p. 89.

2 Department of Education and Science. *Building Bulletin 35: Middle Schools*. H.M.S.O., 1966, p. 3.

3 Central Advisory Council for Education. *Half Our Future* (Newsom Report), H.M.S.O., 1963, p. 119.

4 West Riding of Yorkshire Education Department, *The Organisation of Education in Certain Areas of the West Riding*, 1963.

Further reading

ALLPORT, GORDON W., *Pattern and Growth in Personality*, Holt, Rinehart & Winston, 1963.

BERLYNE, D. E., 'Recent developments in Piaget's work', *Brit. J. Educ. Psych.*, 26 (1), 1957.

BRUNER, J. S., *The Process of Education*, Harvard University Press, 1960.

DOLL, E. A., *The Measurement of Social Competence: A Manual for the Vineland Social Maturity Scale*. Educ. Test. Bureau. Minneapolis, 1953.

EVANS, K. M., *Sociometry and Education*, Routledge, 1965.

FRASER, E., *Home Environment and the School*, Scottish Council for Research in Education, No. 43, University of London Press, 1959.

FREIDLANDER, B. Z., 'A psychologist's second thoughts on concepts, curiosity and discovery in teaching and learning', *Harvard Educational Review*, 35 (II), 1965.

HAVIGHURST, R. J. and NEUGARTEN, B. L., *Society and Education*, Allyn & Bacon, 1959.

KEMP, LESLIE, C. D., 'Environmental and other characteristics determining attainment in primary schools', *Brit. J. Educ. Psych.*, 25 (2), 1955.

LYNN, R., 'Temperamental characteristics related to disparity in reading and arithmetic', *Brit. J. Educ. Psych.*, 27 (1), 1957.

LEWIS, M. M., *Language, Thought and Personality in Infancy and Childhood*, Harrap,, 1963.

LURIA, A. R., and YUDOVITCH, F. la., *Speech and the Development of Mental Processes in the Child*, Staples Press, 1959.

LURIA, A. R., *The Role of Speech in the Regulation of Normal and Abnormal Behaviour*, Pergamon Press, 1961.

MCCLELLAND, D. C., *et al.*, *The Achievement Motive*, Appleton Century, 1953.

MCKELLER, P., *Imagination and Thinking: a Psychological Analysis*, Cohen & West, 1957.

MACCOBY, E., NEWCOMBE, T. M. and HARTLEY, E. G., *Readings in Social Psychology*, Methuen, 1958.

MAYS, J. B., *Education and the Urban Child*, Liverpool University Press, 1962.

MUSGROVE, F., *The Family, Education and Society*, Routledge, 1966.

MUSSEN, P. H., *The Psychological Development of the Child*, Prentice-Hall, 1963.

NATIONAL ASSOCIATION FOR MENTAL HEALTH, *Periods of Stress in the Primary School*, London.

PALMER, R., *Science in the Primary School*, Ministry of Education, Pamphlet No. 2, H.M.S.O., 1962.

PARSONS, T. and BALES, R. F., *Family: Socialisation and Interaction Process*, Routledge, 1956.

PEEL, E. A., *The Pupil's Thinking*, Oldbourne, 1960.

PIAGET, J., *The Language and Thought of the Child*, Routledge, 1959.

PIAGET, J., *The Child's Conception of Number*, Routledge, 1952.

STAINES, J. W., 'The self picture as a factor in the classroom', *Brit. J. Educ. Psych.*, 27 (2), 1958.

TANNER, J. M. and INHELDER, B., eds., *Discussions on Child Development*, Tavistock Publications, 1956, vol. 1.

TORRANCE, P., *The Nature of Creativity*. Prentice-Hall, 1963.

VERNON, M. D., *The Psychology of Perception*, University of London Press, 1965.

VERNON, P. E., *Personality Tests and Assessments*, Methuen, 1962.

VYGOTSKY, L., *Thought and Language*, Wiley, 1962.

YATES, A., ed., *Grouping in Education*. Wiley for UNESCO, 1966.

YATES, A., and PIDGEON, D. A., 'Effects of streaming', *Educational Research*, 2, N.F.E.R., 1965.

Index